The Practitioner Inquiry Series

Marilyn Cochran-Smith and Susan L. Lytle, SERIES EDITORS

(continued)

TEACHER
RESEARCH
for
BETTER
SCHOOLS

Marian M. Mohr
Courtney Rogers
Betsy Sanford
Mary Ann Nocerino
Marion S. MacLean
Sheila Clawson

Foreword by **Ann Lieberman**

Teachers College,
Columbia University
New York and London

National Writing Project
University of California
Berkeley, California

Copublished by Teachers College Press, 1234 Amsterdam Avenue, New York, NY 10027 and the National Writing Project, 2105 Bancroft Way, Berkeley, CA 94720-1042

Library of Congress Cataloging-in-Publication Data

Teacher research for better schools / Marian M. Mohr . . . [et al.].
    p. cm. — (The practitioner inquiry series)
    Includes bibliographical references (p.) and index.
    ISBN 0-8077-4417-4 — ISBN 0-8077-4418-2 (cloth)
        1. Action research in education—United States. 2. School improvement programs—United States. I. Mohr, Marian M. II.Series
    LB1028.24.T37 2004
    370'.7'2—dc22   2003061064

ISBN 0-8077-4417-4 (paper)
ISBN 0-8077-4418-2 (cloth)

Printed on acid-free paper
Manufactured in the United States of America

11 10 09 08 07 06 05 04   8 7 6 5 4 3 2 1

Contents

Part III.
How Does Teacher Research Affect Schools?

Part IV.
What Does Teacher Research in Schools Mean
to the Educational Community?

Foreword

In this era of quick fixes and prescriptions presumed to enhance teacher learning, it is very refreshing to see an alternative point of view posited—a view that puts teachers at the center of their own learning. In a lucid, straightforward, and insightful way, the authors of *Teacher Research for Better Schools* take us on a journey through the classrooms of several of the authors, teaching us about what they learned when they began to inquire into their own practice.

We learn that when teachers do research they seek to be "rigorous and respectful of the research tradition;" however, their research is not distanced, but instead is passionate about its utility to better shape their own classrooms and to influence others as well. It is this "collaborative knowledge building" that aims to transform schools from the inside-out, rather than the other way around. And this, some of us believe, is the difference between real or superficial change.

We learn that when teachers are encouraged to inquire into their own classrooms, they look to other researchers to help them think about learning and teaching and to theorize about their own work. This reading of other researchers, coupled with questions about their teaching, helps them formulate their own theories. While being respectful of the research community, these teachers are learning to respect their own work as well as the descriptions of their teaching problems. Going public with their questions and working together to collect evidence is another big step that eventually leads them to take the leap and do their own piece of research.

The questions that teachers ask are as wide ranging as the methods they use:

What happens when chemistry is taught in heterogeneous groups?
What happens when students choose their own spelling words?
How do first graders learn number facts?
What is teaching and learning from the student's perspective?

We learn not only how teachers think and what problems they deem worthy of study, but how these teacher researchers teach. We learn the multitude of strategies and approaches these teachers use as they become more conscious of themselves as an important tool in the learning process, and as they collect and analyze data in their own classrooms.

But doing teacher research for these authors is not just a solitary process for individuals to learn about their practice, it is also about how relationships between teachers and their principals become better understood and enacted. In the final analysis, teacher researchers help build a more reciprocal relationship, encouraging principals to support teachers' efforts and teachers to better understand the complexities of the larger school context and its organization. In the process, both teacher researchers and principals come to trust one another and to make public the tensions that each feels in working through their new relationships in their school cultures. The knowledge they generate together helps make possible the support that teachers need to carry on their research and a better understanding of how principals could use these research communities to strengthen the instruction in their schools.

This journey describing a group of teacher researchers sensitively documents the elusive role of leadership by teachers. How do teachers lead in a profession that often insists on a view of egalitarianism? What is the role of a teacher who plays both "insider" and "outsider"? How do teachers build credibility with their peers that allows them to overcome the tension produced by being in a different role? These questions as well as several others are explored while describing the particulars of the role of teacher leadership and the important struggle to be both a peer and colleague—as well as one who moves the issues and conversation forward. In short, to be a teacher knowing when to intervene and when to be quiet; how to make suggestions without undermining the teachers' own knowledge. These are significant relationships to build and demand a real sensitivity and practice in learning how to work collaboratively and to lead at the same time.

As the journey continues, the teacher researchers form a network that binds the teachers together in a collective organization that supports their work. Like all other networks, it is loose, flexible, important, and tenuous. Agendas are created according to the needs of its participants. Sometimes the talk is about teacher research; other times it is about support or the need for policies that enable teachers in leading their own development. But whatever it is, it brings people together to further their work and provides a forum for learning, teaching, problem posing, and problem solving—a kind of teacher development that gets to the heart of teaching problems as they are experienced and lived.

These researchers extend teacher research beyond the classroom to include its influences on the school, its support at the district level, its necessity as part of a graduate program and/or course, its uses as part of school planning, and more. As we take this journey with the authors, the book teaches us what it means to be a member of a professional learning community. From the start, teachers become researchers by doing research; they become teacher leaders by creating learning opportunities for other teachers; they become colleagues by shaping a new role for themselves and their principals. They become both learners and teachers, turning private conversations into public forums; studying their own and others' learning processes; and creating a network to assure continuance and support for their efforts at changing their practice and their schools. In these authors' hands we have, at last, a book that goes beyond teacher research as a professional development tool and shows us how teachers can both produce knowledge as well as consume it. It is this kind of professional knowledge that will both improve the quality of teaching and transform schools. And it is this kind of book that can be used as a primer to help make it happen.

—Ann Lieberman
Visiting Professor at Stanford University and Senior Scholar at the
Carnegie Foundation for the Advancement of Teaching

Preface

The central idea of this book is that support of teacher research in schools promotes a school culture with student and teacher learning at its center. By "support" we mean respect for teachers' professionalism as they conduct classroom research, work collaboratively, develop teacher research networks, and disseminate their findings. By "a culture of student and teacher learning" we mean that all parts of a school or district program—curriculum, testing, extracurricular activities—are derived from and secondary to teacher and student learning.

These ideas are the result of our research. As teacher researchers, we collected and analyzed data in tapes, notebooks, and files. But we recognized as we wrote drafts of this book that our excitement in communicating what we were finding out differed from the more detached observations that our research required of us. We were eager for action. We wrote from a solid base in research and analysis, but also from a position of advocacy.

In each part of the book we address a general question:

Part I. What leads to teacher research in schools?
Part II. What happens when teachers conduct teacher research?
Part III. How does teacher research affect schools?
Part IV. What does teacher research in schools mean to the educational community?

We raised questions, collected data, and re-asked questions or revised them. We sought new understandings from our data analysis. We offer these understandings—our learning—to our readers because we believe that research teaches us by providing an understanding of the experiences of others.

We have two additional reasons for recording and sharing what we learned. First, we want to add the voices of K–12 teacher researchers to the discussions that are taking place in the profession. Our voices reflect our background as classroom and resource teachers, staff developers and curriculum planners, middle-level administrators and, above all, as teacher researchers working together. Second, we want to present our ideas to an audience beyond our teacher researcher colleagues—to educators, reformers, parents, and administrators searching for ways to make our schools better places for learning.

Although we had had much experience in teacher research and had worked together on many occasions, we had to learn about composing a book collaboratively. We wrote individually about our own research studies that were conducted with the help of colleagues in the schools. We also wrote chapters to which we all contributed, for example, the chapter about our background knowledge (Chapter 2).

A Spencer Foundation grant enabled us to write together over the period of a year and a half. We are also grateful to the U.S. Office of Educational Research and Improvement, Fund for the Improvement and Reform of Schools and Teaching, for funds to conduct the study. The Office of Educational Planning Services, Fairfax County (Virginia) Public Schools, supported us in carrying out the grant project.

Much has happened in our schools since the beginning of this project, but by far the worst was the death of Marvin Spratley, the principal of the high school in the teacher research project. He was a supporter from the earliest days and fully understood the value and impact of having a teacher research group in his school. When asked in a public forum what he thought was valuable about teacher research, he said, "I saw right away that it grew out of teachers' desire to improve students' learning." He supported teacher researchers, read their work, and used their findings in his own work. We had the utmost respect for him as an educator and administrator and miss him very much. We dedicate our book to him.

MARIAN M. MOHR
COURTNEY ROGERS
BETSY SANFORD
MARY ANN NOCERINO
MARION S. MACLEAN
SHEILA CLAWSON

TEACHER
RESEARCH
for
BETTER
SCHOOLS

What Leads to Teacher Research in Schools?

Part I establishes the background for our argument that teacher research in schools encourages student and teacher learning. We explain the planning, thinking, and defining of our perspective. We describe how our theories and definitions evolved from our background as K–12 teachers and why that context matters.

The first chapter follows our journey as teacher researchers and coordinators of teacher research groups. We describe the way our teacher research project was conceived—why it was planned the way it was—and how it was supported. The second chapter brings together the experiences, discussions, and readings from which we built the theories of learning, teaching, and educational change that underlie our concept of teacher research in schools. The third chapter is our definition of teacher research based on those theories.

CHAPTER 1

Our Journey: Supporting Teacher Research in Schools

Courtney Rogers

The value ... of doing research is to figure out, to know what it is as you're going along.

—Mary Ann Nocerino

As the subway car stopped to let passengers off and on and gathered speed again, I glanced up from my reading to see that I had missed my stop and connecting train and was now headed in the wrong direction. It was the week between Christmas and New Year's, and I was on my way to meet my colleague, Marian Mohr, who waited in her car in the snow and ice-filled Metro parking lot. Mohr and I were drafting a proposal for a U.S. Department of Education grant to support a teacher researcher project. We had responses from our colleagues to an earlier draft and a deadline that was fast approaching.

At the next stop, I got off, boarded a train in the opposite direction, and continued rereading the draft I was carrying, trying to make every minute count. Finally I arrived at the right station, waved to Mohr, and before long we were safe and warm in her living room, immersed in the proposal writing and determined to have it ready to share with our colleagues when they returned from their holiday leave. The proposal would outline our next steps in the journey that we had begun together as teacher researchers some years before and would, we believed, be important for teachers and students in schools across our district.

EMBARKING

The project we were proposing was based on work we had been doing for nearly 15 years. We had been supporting teacher researchers in several elementary, middle, and high schools and in several cross-school groupings. While their work was not widely recognized in our district, evidence of its

3

presence had stubbornly broken ground—in publications, an annotated bibliography, and an article in the district's magazine. In designing this proposal we were trying to identify the next logical steps to strengthen our district's teacher research efforts.

From their inception, the proposal and the project it described were a collaborative effort. The proposal itself was shaped primarily by Mohr, Mary Ann Nocerino (my office colleague), and me, with the help and advice of a few other colleagues. Each of us had a history of participation in teacher research. Mohr, a high school teacher, had designed and led a graduate-level teacher researcher seminar and had worked with many groups of teacher researchers over the years. Nocerino and I, working out of the same central office, had supported teacher research school-based groups. The three of us were committed to working with the project, should it be funded.

In our initial discussions, we had identified our assumptions and the principles that we believed to be important to the project. We saw teacher research as a way of knowing; we viewed it as a process that allowed teachers to build knowledge about their students' learning and about their own practice. Our research experiences and those of our colleagues had taught us that teacher research could lead to new theories and revised practice in classrooms.

We also believed that knowledge is built collaboratively within schools. We wanted to shape the project to give teachers support as they conducted research with their colleagues and used the resulting knowledge to inform decisions about classroom teaching and learning, curriculum and school programs, and, ultimately, school policies. It would be a project led by teacher researchers themselves, transforming classrooms and schools from the inside out. The role of the central office would be one of support and facilitation rather than of direction and mandate.

From our combined experiences, we had identified certain forms of institutional support that could benefit school-based teacher researcher groups:

- *An Experienced Teacher Researcher Leader.* We knew that teacher leaders could help new and veteran researchers through a research process, facilitate group meetings in which teacher researchers provide support for one another, and oversee administrative tasks related to the group's functioning.
- *Opportunities for Collaboration.* We recognized the fundamental importance of collaboration among the teacher researchers within their own school group and across school groups when the opportunity was available.

- *Time.* We had witnessed repeatedly that time to meet together was a crucial element to teacher researchers. In the past, teachers had benefited from being granted substitute leave time so that they could work with their colleagues. We had also considered how reduced teaching duties for teacher leaders would help them carry out responsibilities related to supporting their groups.
- *Support for Writing and Publishing.* We believed that writing was an important tool for both conducting research and disseminating the findings, and that dissemination of teacher research could play a part in improving instruction. Support for writing and publication included help with revising and editing research report drafts as well as providing clerical support and funding sources for printing and publishing the reports.
- *Recognition of Teacher Research.* We recognized how important it was to help teacher researchers consider ways to present their findings to their colleagues within their schools and beyond and, on the other hand, to encourage nonclassroom educators to understand and promote the value of the work.
- *Support of the Principal.* We had also learned that when teacher research flourished in schools, a key factor was the principal's support for the teacher researchers' efforts. Principals had to recognize that the time teachers devoted to their research was important to their continued learning and professional growth and ultimately to the students they taught.

PROPOSING A PROJECT DESIGN

Based on these understandings from our past experiences and propelled by the looming deadline, Mohr and I reviewed the recommendations of our colleagues and began to clarify the components of the project we were proposing. We ignored the snowstorm outside as we cut and pasted the pieces of the proposal together. The project design now included three components:

School-Based Teacher Researcher Groups

At the heart of the project would be groups of teacher researchers in three schools, working together to conduct research on their teaching and the learning of their students. Each school would have a teacher researcher leader, who would teach half of the time and coordinate teacher research in the school and among the three project schools for the other half. Like their colleagues, the teacher leaders would conduct classroom research. The school groups would meet regularly to refine and focus research questions; discuss, analyze, and interpret data; and write reports of their research. While we expected that membership in each school-based group would change from year to year, we hoped that some teachers would participate all 3 years.

In each of the three schools selected there existed a diverse student population, a principal supportive of teacher leadership, and an experienced teacher researcher to lead the group. Betsy Sanford, teaching first grade at Lemon Road Elementary School, had conducted research and had worked with colleagues to lead the teacher researcher seminar. Sheila Clawson, an English teacher at Poe Middle School, had conducted teacher research, worked with teacher groups, and held various leadership positions as a classroom teacher. Marion MacLean, a Falls Church High School English teacher and teacher researcher, had conducted research studies, led teacher researcher groups and, with Mohr, had coauthored a guide for conducting teacher research. As teacher leaders within their schools, Sanford, Clawson, and MacLean would play key roles in supporting their school groups.

The Planning Group

The second component of the project would be a Planning Group made up of the three school-based teacher researcher leaders, Sanford, Clawson, and MacLean; the two middle-level administrators, Nocerino and Rogers; and Mohr, who had just retired from classroom teaching and would serve as school liaison. The Planning Group would oversee the project all 3 years and make decisions about how to support the school-based groups. The group would also work with the school groups, school-based administrators, and the district's central administration, helping secure district resources and providing ways for the three school groups to work together.

The Teacher Researcher Network

The third major component of the project grew out of our commitment to district-level connection among the teacher researchers in the three project schools and other teacher researchers across the district. We envisioned a structure, eventually called the Teacher Researcher Network, to support this larger community of teacher researchers. Members of the Network would be experienced teacher researcher leaders who could identify ways to publicize the work of teacher rearchers, promote systemwide support, help guide policy related to teacher research, and participate in professional networks beyond the district. Research findings and information about teacher research and leadership would be disseminated through the Network and through school publications, presentations, a regional teacher researcher conference, and other professional conferences and publications.

These three components, interconnected, became the framework of the 3-year project as we described it in the proposal. Mohr and I melded the pieces together and over the next few weeks, with the help of our colleagues, revised and refined the proposal. We submitted it, hopeful but less than confident, and returned to our various responsibilities and our individual professional journeys.

GETTING UNDERWAY

In June we were notified that we had been awarded the grant. Faced with beginning the project in September, the Planning Group began meeting immediately. As leaders and participants, we expected to direct the project, but we would also study systematically what happened as it unfolded. We would conduct the project research in collaboration with the teacher researchers in the schools. What we learned would inform not only our own work but also, we hoped, the work of other interested teacher researcher communities and school systems.

At the early meetings we worked to get the project off the ground and sought ways to operate both collaboratively and efficiently. In addition, as researchers, we struggled to figure out what was most important to pay attention to. Mohr, mentioning the interviews we had begun with the project's school principals, said, "I have this horrible sense that data is leaking away." In response came light laughter and agreeing nods. We all knew that data could be elusive and that we were part of our data. As we continued to talk, we acknowledged the need to analyze data as we proceeded. Nocerino reminded us that "the value of doing research is to figure out, to know what it is, as you're going along."

Eventually we reached consensus about the research for the project. The three teacher leaders would help to collect and analyze data about the project, but their primary research would be conducted in their own classrooms. We knew from experience how important their classroom research was to their role in supporting their fellow teacher researchers. The Planning Group members without classrooms would each assume responsibility for some aspect of the overall project research.

Mohr planned to look at teacher researchers' teaching, and Nocerino was interested in what kind of leaders teacher researchers might be and become. My research would focus on the network of teacher researchers and its connections to the Planning Group and the working of the project as a whole. We knew, however, that additional research questions would emerge as the project unfolded, and that we would follow those that seemed most compelling and important to our understanding of our over-arching question: What happens when teacher researchers conduct research in their schools?

Our journey together was well underway. While we knew there would be unexpected twists and turns along the way, we had collective experience and faith in a process for constructing knowledge together that would steady our course. The destination, although uncertain, was full of promise. We had nowhere to go but forward.

CHAPTER 2

Out of Our Experience: Useful Theory

Generating a theory involves a process of research.
—Barney Glaser and Anselm Strauss

When a teacher remarked during a teacher researcher group discussion, "Theory is only useful if it's *useful*," we all knew what she meant. Theory often seems the last thing needed in a classroom; it seems esoteric, over-generalized, and unrelated to the practice of teaching. A useful theory, on the other hand, can be a way to see the myriad experiences—the data of a teacher's life—in a coherent way. Barney Glaser and Anselm Strauss (1967) call this "grounded theory" because it is based on data. Betsy Sanford calls it an "organizing principle," a framework from which to try out new practices and collect new data.

As teachers, we developed our own theories daily as we taught, and they were constantly revised and adapted as a result of our experiences. We felt excitement when we read a theorist who saw the classroom world the way we did, but we were as likely to add that theory to our own theoretical construct ("He thinks the way I've been thinking") as to feel legitimized by the theory of a more famous researcher or theorist ("My theory is validated by his").

Discovering the origins of a teacher's theories is therefore problematic. As with most teacher researchers, our theory building emerged from a complex mix of classroom experiences, collegial exchanges, reflective opportunities, and selected reading. We did not trace each of our theories to a bibliographical source although we meant no disrespect by our method, and we were not constrained by the theory building conventions of the academic community. Instead, we were free to explore and connect ideas that were important to us in the company of our colleagues and within the context of our classrooms.

This chapter is a description of our most important theories and the journey of discovery that led to their development. We describe our theories of learning, of the relationship of teaching to learning, and of educational change because they form the foundation for our ideas about teacher research in schools. At the end of each background description is a summary of our theories. After discussing the theories, we relate them to our methods and then to the ideas of our colleagues in the field of teacher research.

HOW STUDENTS AND TEACHERS LEARN

Mary Ann Nocerino describes her learning process by drawing ideas from two articles from the professional literature:

> When I observe the moon wax and wane in the night sky, I feel an excitement, seeded by Duckworth's article "Teaching as Research" (1986), about learning—my own and my students'—the knowledge that through careful observation and questioning, I can learn about whatever I choose—and maybe make sense of it but not always.
>
> Janet Emig's theory of nonmagical thinking ["magical thinking" is the notion that children learn because teachers teach, and only what teachers teach] in *The Web of Meaning* (1983) freed me to observe and question what students might be learning. This research approach to learning became instilled in me as a way of being—a way of approaching many things in my professional and personal life.

Nocerino derived the ideas of observing and questioning—what she calls a "research approach" to life—from her reading of Duckworth and Emig. As a group, we all see research as our way of learning.

To the idea of research as learning, Courtney Rogers adds the use of writing to learn:

> I have learned the most when I was conducting research with the support of other teacher researchers who respond to my talking and writing as I develop questions; collect, analyze, and interpret data; and try to articulate findings and implications. My writing and my colleagues' responses to it have been especially critical.

As a group, we also agree that our habits of journal writing, writing to learn, and writing together are basic to our ideas about learning.

Donald Graves gave us copies of articles he and his colleagues drafted *as* they were conducting research on the writing of elementary school students. These articles included one by Mary Ellen Giacobbe (1981), the first article we recognized as teacher research. Graves and his colleagues demonstrated for us both writing about research in progress and writing "deadline drafts." We adapted his ways of writing about research to our own context, and his struggles with writing taught us to value our own.

Donald Murray, Graves's colleague, became our colleague as well. His article "Write Research to Be Read" (1982) freed us from the kind of research writing that we had composed in graduate classes and read in professional journals, and supported our idea that classroom data could be written about in interesting ways without diminishing its validity.

These university colleagues helped us clarify our ideas about writing to learn and see what we were doing in our classrooms in a larger context. There were also K–12 teachers and colleagues, whose learning experiences mirrored ours.

Anne Wotring (Wotring & Tierney, 1981), a member of the earliest research group in our area, was a high school English teacher when she enrolled in a chemistry class that was learning with the use of writing—what she ended up calling "think writing." From her research we began to value the role of participant-observer and to use "think writing" in our own work.

Mary Schulman (1987) was interested in the findings of Graves's work on children's writing. She showed us how she learned by analyzing her elementary school students' writing. Each year she continued her research, working toward better understandings, and showed us that learning as a researcher is a continuous process of revision and reanalysis.

Bernadette Glaze (1987), a high school history teacher, wrote about her research on writing to learn history. She made the I-search ideas of Ken Macrorie (1980) legitimate to us and showed us that they aren't, as she put it, "I-search anything, they are just plain research."

Bob Ingalls and Joyce Jones (1993), building both a school-based staff development program and a longitudinal study of high school students' writing, kept the principles of respect for teacher knowledge and the importance of learning from students at the center of their efforts. We saw their research as demonstrating how learning with colleagues takes place.

Much of our learning has been with teacher colleagues and accounts for our belief in research group members learning with and from each other. Sheila Clawson and Sharon Gerow team-taught a social studies/English class at a middle school.

Clawson: I would have to say the most influential person for me is Sharon Gerow (1997)—there is nothing like watching someone day after day modeling the strategies of teacher research. I wasn't even aware of what they were, but I began to imitate them. Seeing them demonstrated in the classroom and talking about what is going on with someone who is there all the time was a slow realization that I was becoming a researcher.

Betsy Sanford elaborates on this idea, discussing the influence of the Planning Group:

> Without question, the people I have learned the most from are this group. . . . First, it was always within a context. We were always wrestling with the philosophical and methodological issues of teacher research within the context of real groups that were really operating. Second, the discussion was ongoing. The issues surfaced and resurfaced, sometimes in slightly different forms, so that we were forced to address them repeatedly.

Sanford's description of our way of learning together shows both its ongoing nature and its context dependence.

We summarize our theories of learning as follows:

> As learners and researchers, teachers and students are involved in a process of discovery and construction. Oral and written language promote and enable learning. Learning takes place within a context—a group of teachers or students and teachers in a classroom—and this context is itself situated within a larger societal context, both influencing teaching and learning.

HOW TEACHING AND LEARNING ARE RELATED

What we assumed to be true about learning was closely connected to what we believed to be true about teaching. Marion MacLean describes this connection:

> I first read Mina Shaughnessy's *Errors and Expectations* (1977) in 1981 around the time I went through the Writing Project. I'd been noticing in my classroom things that didn't fit or make sense: I was doing my best to make things work out in a particular way, but the more I tried, the worse it got. What I saw in M.S.'s work was her embracing the problem—welcoming it as a puzzle—a happy puzzle because of the assumption that logic was at work. Errors were not violations of principles. Errors were sudden flashes of light that could—if you knew how to value them—lead to understanding the principles at work.

As MacLean does above, we began to define teaching as a process of research.

Magdalene Lampert (1985) added another dimension to our thinking with her concept of teaching as "managing dilemmas" rather than solving problems. Marian Mohr describes Lampert's influence:

> Her article was one of my first experiences with the *Harvard Education Review*. Here was an elementary school teacher researcher who was also a university professor researcher. I made copies and took it to the teacher researcher seminar that evening. It came at a time when we were weary, and conceptualizing our work as unsolvable dilemmas, while it could have been discouraging, lifted our spirits. We could see what happened in our classrooms as "data," not as sinister plots to make our lives miserable!

Teaching and learning were connected for us by Lampert's concept. We could not control our lives or the lives of our students, but we could encourage learning by the way we managed and defined teaching and learning in our classrooms. We could learn to understand what was going on.

Lawrence Stenhouse's (1985) ideas led us to think about the effects of teacher research on curriculum and professional development. Our classroom observations affected our classroom curriculum. Our yearlong research process was like a graduate course; our understandings based on our research were professional development for each other.

Probably our most important influence in the field of teaching and professional development was the National Writing Project (Gray, 2000). Don Gallehr (1987), director of the Northern Virginia Writing Project (NVWP) at George Mason University (GMU) where we were all "teacher-consultants," learned about teacher research along with us. His openness to learning from us contributed to our thinking about learning from our students and also from teacher colleagues.

Nocerino and Rogers both wrote about the influence of the NVWP.

Nocerino: NVWP was an important professional experience for me. As part of my teaching, I taped first graders reading their writing aloud and learned some interesting things about self-correction and revision. I used some of the data as part of the presentation I prepared for the Summer Institute. The presentation provided for me a connection between my teaching and teacher research.

Rogers: I remember my amazement at reading Janet Emig's (1971) research on the composing processes of twelfth graders during the

NVWP Summer Institute. That she had actually looked at and documented what students do when they write—*as they write*—seemed so logical and so unusual. Even though it involved tape recorders and a substantial time commitment, something like it was not totally out of the realm of possibility for me as a high school teacher. I realized how little the so-called experts knew about what students actually do when they compose in writing. And as far as I was concerned, Emig was headed in the right direction for finding out.

Through professional development opportunities sponsored by NVWP, we talked with various university researchers in the field of writing research and learned how they approached the world as researchers.

Mohr: I remember meeting Dixie Goswami. She wore a loose shirt with a big tiger printed on it. She was outspoken, had a large laugh, a deep southern accent. She respected the work of teachers. "When you become a researcher, you cease to be a victim of fads." "Any piece of research is theory building." "Somebody else has to be able to make sense of your data." Those are three quotes from the first time I heard her talk. I think what I got from her, though, beyond the specific ideas, was an attitude. Teacher research can and should be done.

The National Writing Project (NWP) model flew in the face of most of the professional development we had experienced. We were used to knowledge received from outsiders—"what works" and "research says" mantras coupled with an absence of appreciation for our experience and thinking. From the NWP we learned to respect our own adaptations of the work of outside researchers rather than try to replicate them. Respect for the learner became part of our theory of teaching children and adults.

Sanford: As a teacher researcher in the field of emergent mathematics learning, I have valued the work of Kathy Richardson. When I attended a session by her at a National Council of Teachers of Mathematics annual meeting, she mentioned conducting research in problem solving. I spoke to her at the break, noting that I had been involved in problem-solving research as well. Her instant reaction was to ask, "Well, what are you finding out?" She treated me as a fellow researcher.

Respect for the learner in a teaching-learning situation is complicated, and we were aware that our lives and the lives of our students and colleagues were different in many ways. Because all six of us are white, native English-speaking, and women, we had long worked, as teachers, to become better informed about the diversity of our students and colleagues. We knew that social and cultural influences were always present in our research as well as our classrooms.

We studied the work of researcher James Comer (1980), who was also interested in the school as an inclusive learning community, and Gloria Ladson-Billings (1994), who was also interested in how teaching and learning interact in a classroom of racial differences. We learned as well from teacher researcher colleagues such as Renee Moore (1998), who was also interested in language learning and achievement. Researcher Concha Delgado-Gaitan (1993), who was interested in how participating in a community and studying that same community could be both ethical and valid, expanded our vision of our position as teacher researchers in our schools. In James Banks's (1998) descriptions of "indigenous-insiders" and "external-insiders," we saw ourselves as teacher researchers on the fringes of some and indigenous to other educational communities.

As we reached out for the ideas of colleagues, Judith Warren Little (1991) gave us an understanding of professional isolation and its effect on our schools and teaching.

> *Rogers*: By the time I knew about her work, it was confirming what I knew through my experience. The collegial relationships she described that countered the professional isolation so prevalent in schools were alive and well among my colleague teacher researchers. I remember the high school teachers in the first teacher research group I helped lead commenting with some amazement that it was the first school experience they'd had of honest professional dialogue with "colleagues" about the teaching and learning in their classrooms, not the teacher lounge "war stories" or laments about poor student behavior or performance but stories about teaching and learning episodes that helped them understand what was happening in their classrooms.

We saw that the daily stuff of the classroom, the work of students and teachers, is valuable data about teaching and learning and can be interpreted by teachers and students given the opportunity. We summarize our theories about teaching as it is related to learning as follows:

> Teachers (and their students) can and do study teaching and learning as they teach and learn. Teachers who conduct classroom research initiate and carry out their own professional development

and learning. When teachers work together to study teaching and learning, they break out of the isolation of the classroom and begin to teach each other.

The more our ideas about teaching and learning developed, the more they pushed us to consider educational change, especially in classrooms and schools.

HOW SCHOOLS CHANGE

Our ideas about educational change are based on teaching and learning as a process of research. That process, although individual, takes place within a context of trusted professional colleagues or "critical friends" (Costa & Kallick, 1993). When we heard the term *critical friends* used for a certain kind of professional relationship—one of mentoring or coaching—we coupled it with an idea from Matthew Miles and Michael Huberman (1994). The validity of qualitative research, they assert, is enhanced by the number of research colleagues who examine the data critically and whose responses are incorporated into the understandings being developed by the researcher.

These two ideas reflected our experience in small research response groups. We knew the groups assisted teacher researchers in speaking freely about their teaching, and we began to see a combination of ideas that made the research group of critical friends essential to the validity of teacher research. It is through questioning and criticizing, agreeing and disagreeing, but with fundamental respect and support for each other, that we interpret and learn from our data.

> *Mohr*: When I opened *Teachers, Their World, and Their Work: Implications for School Improvement* (1984), written by Ann Lieberman and Lynne Miller, I noticed right away its tone of respect and understanding when describing the work of teaching. (I had read many books that advertised a true description of teaching, which seemed way off to me.) When Mary Ann [Nocerino] gave us copies of "Creating Intentional Learning Communities" (1996) by Ann Lieberman, I wanted to read what she had to say. I was excited to discover things in the article that were similar to what we knew from our teacher researcher groups.

Our experiences verified Lieberman's description of school-based learning communities and local networks that allow members to accept the responsibility for their own personal and professional development.

We had read Paolo Freire (1970) to learn about teaching adult students to write, but learned as well from his emphasis on the social and political contexts of learning. Patricia Stock's *The Dialogic Curriculum* (1995), an interpretation of Freire's work for North American classrooms based on teacher research, brought together theories based on the concept of context that made sense with our experience.

The students' context for learning, brought to school from family and community life (including societal inequities), intersects with the classroom context and, in turn, with the teacher's own context. Identifying the interacting contexts forms the basis for building a learning community.

A summary of our ideas about teacher and school change follows:

> Teacher researchers working with colleagues create a learning community within a school that affects student learning, professional development, and school decision making. This community develops because of changes in the way teacher researchers view themselves and others and through the identification of the contexts in which they work together.

RESEARCH METHODS

Because of the experiences we have already described and the theorists and researchers we have mentioned, the research in our schools leaned heavily toward adaptations of qualitative and ethnographic methodology. Some data was analyzed numerically, but no experimental or comparative studies with control groups were conducted. In no way, however, do we limit the use of any kind of methodology by teacher researchers so long as it is used ethically with respect for students and colleagues.

We searched out methods from a variety of fields—sociology, ethnography, psychology, and anthropology—adapting the ideas we learned to our teaching and researching. Evelyn Jacob (1982), a university colleague and ethnographer, answered our questions about ethnography and qualitative research.

> *Rogers*: Evelyn was the first university-based teacher of research methods I met who valued teacher research for its potential contributions to the professional discourse. She said it, but she also lived it as a practicing teacher researcher.

Reading Yvonna Lincoln and Egon Guba (1985) taught us about "naturalistic inquiry." Although they were not writing for teacher researchers,

we saw how classroom teachers might interpret data and develop understandings in the midst of the lively, multivariate classroom.

Mohr: I remember Guba's little blue book called *Toward a
Methodology of Naturalistic Inquiry in Educational Evaluation*
(1978)—sending away for it, reading it, and underlining "premature closure is a cardinal sin and tolerance of ambiguity a
virtue."

Eliot Mishler's "Meaning in Context: Is There Any Other Kind?"
(1979) confirmed for us that classroom context was vital to any understanding of our data. We learned to use and appreciate "thick description" from Clifford Geertz (1973), and it became a byword during
revision sessions for teacher research reports. Shirley Brice Heath
(1983) and Evelyn Jacob (1982) taught us what an ethnography looks
like and also the problems and advantages of being an ethnographer in
a community.

George J. McCall and J. L. Simmons's *Issues in Participant Observation* (1969) included Barney Glaser's "The Constant Comparative Method of Qualitative Analysis." This method seemed particularly well
adapted to a yearlong classroom research study where a teacher could
use the information from an afternoon's analytical comparison of data to
inform the next day's teaching, collecting still more data for continued
analysis.

From Matthew Miles and Michael Huberman (1994) we learned how
qualitative and quantitative data complement each other, which led us to
consider ways that schools might report student achievement with information from teacher research as well as standardized test scores.

We adapted what we learned about methodology from other fields,
but we also learned to value what we already did as teachers and see it
in a different light as researchers. Eliot Eisner (1991) showed us how our
own expertise and knowledge could become a valued part of our
research and challenged us to think of new dissemination and publication forms.

Teacher researcher colleagues who began publishing their studies also
added to our understanding of methodology. Scott Christian's *Exchanging
Lives* (1997), for example, was full of E-mail data, written by his students
to other students in rural areas all over the United States.

Our methods in the research studies included in this book are described
in each study. In this discussion, we wanted to explain the general sources
of our thinking about these methods as they relate to our experience, our
exchanges of ideas with colleagues, and our reading.

EXCHANGES WITH CONTEMPORARIES

We have benefited greatly from connections with our contemporaries who work in the field of teacher research.

Marilyn Cochran-Smith and Susan Lytle in their book *Inside/Outside: Teacher Research and Knowledge* (1993) offered a taxonomy of teacher research that respects the many methods teachers use to reflect on their teaching, including talk and journal writing. By presenting their ideas about teacher research to their university colleagues, they helped us to consider our responsibilities as researchers to take part in the discourse of the educational community.

Glenda Bissex and Richard Bullock in *Seeing for Ourselves: Case Study Research by Teachers of Writing* (1987) published teacher research articles we could compare to the ones we were producing and Bissex's definition started us thinking more about ways of defining teacher research. Our definition in this book owes a debt to hers.

Teacher researchers from our district published in the *Journal of Teacher Research* edited by Ruth Hubbard and Brenda Power. Their book *The Art of Classroom Inquiry* (1993) has been a valuable resource, and we appreciate their emphasis on the practical, the actuality of conducting teacher research in a classroom.

As K–12 teacher researchers began to publish and give conference presentations, we made every effort to learn from them. Nancie Atwell's success with a book-length teacher research study, *In the Middle* (1987), encouraged teacher researchers everywhere. Karen Gallas's (1994) writing about issues of racism, poverty, and anger with sometimes painful honesty was a helpful example of how teacher research examines complex and difficult situations.

Because of our connection to the National Writing Project we became acquainted with teacher researchers in other writing projects with whom we shared our ideas. Mary K. Healy (Barr, D'Arcy, & Healy, 1982), Bob Tierney (Wotring & Tierney, 1981), and Joan Cone (1994) are just a few of the California teacher researchers from whom we learned.

By the time this project began, we knew teacher researchers nationwide in schools at all grade levels and in many different disciplines whom we could E-mail about our work. There were special interest groups for teacher research within professional organizations and teacher research strands in projects focused on other topics such as education in urban settings. Each time one or more of us participated in one of these groups, we brought back to the others what we had learned.

As the field of teacher research grew and we had an increasing number of colleagues with whom to learn, it was apparent to us how much we thought we knew was a result of exchanges with the other teacher researchers. We are grateful for their contributions to the kind of talk and writing that continues to push our thinking and increase our learning.

CONCLUSION

We continue to think of our ideas as developing from our practice into revised versions of our theories. Our work together is research—our approach to administration of programs as well as to teaching. At first we wondered, "Why are our meetings so long?!" Eventually we realized that seeing our work as a research process is how we learn. That fundamental principle keeps us looking for new data and keeps our theories as useful as we can make them.

REFERENCES

Atwell, N. (1987). *In the middle: Writing, reading, and learning with adolescents.* Westport, CT: Heinemann-Boynton/Cook.

Banks, J. (1998). The lives and values of researchers: Implications for educating citizens in a multicultural society. *Educational Researcher, 27*(7), 4–17.

Barr, M., D'Arcy, P., & Healy, M. K. (1982). *What's going on? Language/learning episodes in British and American classrooms, grades 4–13.* Westport, CT: Heinemann-Boynton/Cook.

Bissex, G., & Bullock, R. (1987). *Seeing for ourselves: Case study research by teachers of writing.* Westport, CT: Heinemann-Boynton/Cook.

Christian, S. (1997). *Exchanging lives: Middle school writers online.* Urbana, IL: National Council of Teachers of English.

Cochran-Smith, M., & Lytle, S. L. (1993). *Inside/outside: Teacher research and knowledge.* New York: Teachers College Press.

Comer, J. (1980). *School power: Implications of an intervention project.* New York: Macmillan.

Cone, J. (1994). Appearing acts: Creating readers in a high school English class. *Harvard Educational Review, 64*(4), 450–473.

Costa, A. L., & Kallick, B. (1993). Through the lens of a critical friend. *Educational Leadership, 51*(2), 49–51.

Delgado-Gaitan, C. (1993). Researching change and changing the researcher. *Harvard Educational Review, 63*(4), 389–411.

Duckworth, E. (1986). Teaching as research. *Harvard Educational Review, 56*(4), 481–495.

Eisner, E. (1991). *The enlightened eye: Qualitative inquiry and the enhancement of educational practice.* New York: Macmillan.

Emig, J. (1971). *The composing processes of twelfth graders.* Urbana, IL: National Council of Teachers of English.

Emig, J. (1983). *The web of meaning.* Westport, CT: Heinemann-Boynton/Cook.

Freire, P. (1970). *Pedagogy of the oppressed* (M. Ramos, Trans.). New York: Seabury Press.

Gallas, K. (1994). *The languages of learning.* New York: Teachers College Press.

Gallehr, D. (1987). Assessment in context: Toward a National Writing Project model. *The Quarterly of the National Writing Project, 9*(3), 5–7.

Geertz, C. (1973). *The interpretation of cultures: Selected essays by Clifford Geertz.* New York: Basic Books.

Gerow, S. (1997). *Teacher researchers in school-based collaborative teams: One approach to school reform.* Unpublished doctoral dissertation, Institute for Educational Transformation, George Mason University, Fairfax County, VA.

Giacobbe, M. E. (1981). Kids can write the first week of school. *Learning, 10*(2), 132–133.

Glaser, B. (1969). The constant comparative method of qualitative analysis. In G. McCall & J. Simmons (Eds.), *Issues in participant observation: A text and reader* (pp. 216–228). Reading, MA: Addison-Wesley.

Glaser, B. G., & Strauss, A. L. (1967). *The discovery of grounded theory: Strategies for qualitative research.* New York: Aldine.

Glaze, B. (1987). It's not just the writing. In T. Fulwiler (Ed.), *The journal book* (pp. 227–238). Westport, CT: Heinemann-Boynton/Cook.

Goswami, D., & Stillman, P. (Eds.). (1987). *Reclaiming the classroom: Teacher research as an agency for change.* Westport, CT: Heinemann-Boynton/Cook.

Graves, D. (1981). *Writing: Teachers and children at work.* Westport, CT: Heinemann-Boynton/Cook.

Graves, D. (1984). *A researcher learns to write: Selected articles and monographs.* Westport, CT: Heinemann-Boynton/Cook.

Gray, J. (2000). *Teachers at the center.* Berkeley, CA: National Writing Project.

Guba, E. (1978). *Toward a methodology of naturalistic inquiry in educational evaluation.* Los Angeles: Center for the Study of Evaluation, University of California at Los Angeles Graduate School of Education.

Heath, S. B. (1983). *Ways with words: Language, life, and work in communities and classrooms.* New York: Cambridge University Press.

Heath, S. B. (1993). The madness(es) of reading and writing ethnography. *Anthropology and Education Quarterly, 24*(3), 256–268.

Hubbard, R., & Power, B. M. (1993). *The art of classroom inquiry: A handbook for teacher researchers.* Westport, CT: Heinemann-Boynton/Cook.

Ingalls, R., & Jones, J. (1993). Interviewing students about their portfolios. In M. A. Smith & M. Ylvisaker (Eds.), *Teachers' voices: Portfolios in the classroom* (pp. 127–135). Berkeley, CA: National Writing Project.

Jacob, E. (1982). Combining ethnographic and quantitative approaches: Suggestions and examples from a study in Puerto Rico. In P. Gilmore & A. Glatthorn (Eds.), *Children in and out of school: Ethnography and education* (pp. 124–147). Washington, DC: Center for Applied Linguistics.

Ladson-Billings, G. (1994). *The dream keepers: Successful teachers of African American children.* San Francisco: Jossey-Bass.

Lampert, M. (1985). How do teachers manage to teach? Perspectives on problems in practice. *Harvard Educational Review, 55*(2), 178–194.

Lieberman, A. (1996). Creating intentional learning communities. *Educational Leadership, 54*(3), 51–55.

Lieberman, A., & Miller, L. (1984). *Teachers, their world and their work: Implications for school improvement.* Alexandria, VA: Association for Supervision and Curriculum Development.

Lincoln, Y. S., & Guba, E. G. (1985). *Naturalistic inquiry.* Newbury Park, CA: Sage.

Little, J. W. (1991). The persistence of privacy: Autonomy and initiative in teachers' professional relations. *Teachers College Record, 91*(4), 509–536.

Macrorie, K. (1980). *Searching writing.* Westport CT: Heinemann-Boynton/Cook.

Miles, M., & Huberman, A. M. (1994). *Qualitative data analysis: An expanded sourcebook* (2nd ed.). Beverly Hills, CA: Sage.

Mishler, E. G. (1979). Meaning in context: Is there any other kind? *Harvard Educational Review, 19*(1), 1–19.

Moore, R. (1998, Summer). Teaching standard English to African American students: Conceptualizing the research project. *Bread Loaf Rural Teacher Network Magazine* (Middlebury College), 12–15.

Murray, D. (1982). Write research to be read. In *Learning by teaching.* Westport, CT: Heinemann-Boynton/Cook.

Richardson, K. (1999). *Developing number concepts using unifix cubes.* White Plains, NY: Dale Seymour.

Schulman, M. (1987). Reading for meaning: Trying to get past first basal. In M. M. Mohr & M. S. MacLean, *Working together: A guide for teacher researchers* (pp. 111–120). Urbana, IL: National Council of Teachers of English.

Shaughnessy, M. (1977). *Errors and expectations: A guide for the teacher of basic writing.* New York: Oxford.

Stenhouse, L. (1985). *Research as a basis for teaching: Readings from the work of Lawrence Stenhouse* (J. Ruddick & D. Hopkins, eds.). Westport, CT: Heinemann-Boynton/Cook.

Stock, P. L. (1995). *The dialogic curriculum: Teaching and learning in a multicultural society.* Westport, CT: Heinemann-Boynton/Cook.

Wotring, A. M., & Tierney, R. (1981). *Two studies of writing in high school science.* Berkeley, CA: National Writing Project.

CHAPTER 3

Developing a Definition of Teacher Research

Teacher researchers have faith in their students; they know too much to give up on them.

—Marion MacLean

A definition of teacher research began to develop during our journey together and our construction of theories. The definition grew up around six descriptive words intended to acknowledge the conditions, practices, and policies that make teacher research possible, help it flourish, and make its contribution felt in classrooms, schools, and school districts.

We define *teacher research* as inquiry that is *intentional*, *systematic*, *public*, *voluntary*, *ethical*, and *contextual*.

TEACHER RESEARCH IS INTENTIONAL

Teacher researchers begin conducting research by identifying a topic or framing a question they wish to explore and investigate. Teacher research starts with a commitment to examine an aspect of teaching and learning and is carried out through the intentional and systematic collection and analysis of classroom data.

Teacher researchers choose research questions that matter to them. Because they determine their own questions and the course of their research journey based on their own learning needs, their research is responsive to those needs. They may set out in one direction in their research, but their growing understanding of their teaching and their students' learning may lead them to change directions. As their research leads to improved understanding they may revise their plans for the data they collect, the methods they use, and the types of data analysis they conduct. While they cannot predict their research discoveries, they approach each step of the research process with the intention of finding out more about their teaching and their students' learning.

TEACHER RESEARCH IS SYSTEMATIC

Teacher researchers use methods and strategies to document the research process, identify assumptions, collect and analyze both qualitative and quantitative data, and articulate theories, findings, and implications.

Teacher researchers collect a variety of kinds of data to triangulate findings, engage in constant comparison of data they have collected, and check their interpretations with colleagues, students, or parents involved in the study. They respond to challenges to their thinking that other teacher researchers present to them during discussions or in response to drafts of research reports. They formulate theories in relation to their analysis. In these ways, teacher researchers systematically seek to establish an accurate and full picture of a teaching and learning context that will lead to deeper understanding of that context.

TEACHER RESEARCH IS PUBLIC

Although teachers' decisions to conduct research are individually determined, teacher research is a public endeavor. When teachers conduct research, they examine their assumptions, withhold judgments, and look at issues from alternative perspectives in an effort to make apparent to themselves that which has been unseen or silent. They intentionally shift from a private perspective to a more open, public perspective in order to encourage challenges to their understanding. Often, teacher researchers enlist both students and colleagues as co-researchers. They discuss with them their assumptions, their hunches, their data, their methods of data collection, and their data analysis and interpretations throughout the course of the research.

Teachers join in the professional discourse by reporting on their research. Efforts to make their research public involve sharing research processes, findings, and implications with colleagues in their schools and with those in communities beyond their schools through informal exchanges, the publication of research stories and research reports (both in print and on-line), and the presentation of their research at local, national, and international conferences. Teachers conduct research in order to understand better the workings of the classroom or teaching context, and they make their research public in order to add to the body of knowledge about teaching and learning.

TEACHER RESEARCH IS VOLUNTARY

Teacher research is an act that has the potential of risk and vulnerability, requiring that teachers publicly examine their beliefs, assumptions, and understandings related to their teaching practice. Therefore, the decision of whether or not to conduct teacher research remains the teacher's.

While teacher research is voluntary, it is also inclusive. It is conducted by preservice and beginning as well as experienced teachers, and it is of use to all teachers who wish to examine their practice, regardless of their level of expertise about teaching or research. Because teacher research is both voluntary and inclusive, teachers are not evaluated on the basis of whether or not they conduct teacher research nor on the merits of research projects they undertake.

TEACHER RESEARCH IS ETHICAL

Teacher researchers' primary responsibility is to their students, and their students are the primary beneficiaries of their work. They strive to collect data that is representative, often checking with students to confirm the significance and value of the data. They seek student affirmation of their interpretations and acknowledge discrepancies between their interpretations and those of their students.

They invite challenges to their tentative findings by discussing their research with students and colleagues, and they search for additional classroom data that presents confirming or disconfirming perspectives. They obtain permission to quote students or use their work samples, and they are careful to protect information that would compromise the privacy of their students, community members, or colleagues. They report both their successes and their failures, in an attempt to better understand their teaching and the learning of their students.

TEACHER RESEARCH IS CONTEXTUAL

Teacher research requires description of the context for teaching and learning. Rather than attempt to control for variables, teacher researchers strive to define, articulate, and elucidate the context as a whole, to reveal the assumptions at work within the context, and to uncover the connections as well as tensions among elements of that context.

Teacher research both shapes and is shaped by its context. Their research questions reflect teachers' current understanding of their topics, their students, and their teaching context. As teacher researchers gain insight through data collection and analysis, what they learn determines their future research steps. At the same time, they develop new ways of interpreting the events in their classrooms and responding to their students. In turn, those new interpretations and responses can evoke new responses on the part of their students. Teacher research is contextual because it is context-dependent, context-relevant, and context-responsive.

Our description of teacher research developed during our research process as an emerging and shifting understanding. Many teachers contributed. The six key words of the definition, written large on heavy paper, were often hung in a room where teacher research meetings were in progress and referred to as touchstones throughout the discussion.

What Happens When Teachers Conduct Teacher Research?

Part II presents our evidence that teacher research in schools encourages student and teacher learning. Part II takes place in classrooms, during and after school.

In Chapter 4, "The Way I Would Teach: Student Knowledge of Teaching and Learning," student voices describe their understanding of teaching and learning, enabling us to ground our subsequent classroom research in their knowledge. Chapter 5, "It All Adds Up: A Teacher Research Study of Learning Number Facts in First Grade," is one teacher researcher's study of teaching and learning mathematics in her first-grade classroom. It exemplifies the many studies conducted by the teachers in the project.

Chapter 6, "Paying Attention in a Different Way: How Teacher Researchers Teach," presents narratives from teacher researchers' classrooms and interpretations of those narratives by the teachers and the researcher. Chapter 7, "Coming into Focus: How Teacher Researchers Learn," highlights interviews with three teacher researchers and depicts a teacher research group in a school as they learn together.

CHAPTER 4

The Way I Would Teach: Student Knowledge of Teaching and Learning

Marian M. Mohr

I would ask the person questions and see if they have any questions for me. This is the way I would teach.
—a middle school student

As a classroom teacher researcher, I asked my students questions about their learning. Their answers provided information I needed and I developed respect for their knowledge about learning. In my new role as a teacher researcher in others' classrooms, I needed to discover what the students knew about teaching. Before I began observing the teaching and learning of the students and their teachers—my plan for the future—I wanted to answer the question: What do students know about teaching and learning? Conducting this research would also be an introduction to the students and their teachers.

The importance of student thinking to my research went beyond their contributions to my understanding. I was striving for a careful handling of the connections between the researcher and the researched. I believed in Yvonna Lincoln's (1995) statements about the close relationship between ethics and rigor in standards for qualitative research. The more honest and responsive I was in my relationship with these students and their teachers, I believed, the more potential value my research would have.

But what if students were unaware of how teaching works? Would they be able to connect teaching and learning? I would be asking them to start out with metacognition, rather than move toward it. What could I ask that would give me a basis for understanding my observations in their classrooms?

The students ranged from kindergarten to Grade 12 and were in 19 different classrooms. I decided to ask them to assume the role of a teacher rather than to report on teachers they had known. I started with the question, "If you wanted to teach somebody something, how would you do it?" I also suggested, "Tell me the story of a time when you taught somebody something." After they wrote in answer to my questions, we talked, and I took notes on what they said. When our discussion ended, I read back what I had written to see if I had it right.

PRINCIPLES OF TEACHING

As I collected the data, I studied and categorized the students' ideas into three principles of teaching:

1. Be patient.
2. Make learning fun.
3. Don't be boring.

I had heard these principles, often stated less politely, from my own students. But, as I gathered more data, with time to reflect on their stories and statements, I became interested in the way they described the principles in action. Even students in kindergarten and first grade had preferred teaching methods. Their methods were based on their understanding of teaching as interactive and reciprocal between teachers and students and on learning as a part of life itself, not just relegated to schools.

Be Patient

Being patient was the most frequently mentioned behavior necessary to their teaching. A high school student described his way of teaching this way:

1. Practice
2. Patiently
3. Slowly
4. Nicely
5. Calmly
6. Efficiently
7. One step at a time

Patience included trying to teach in different ways. "If a teacher explains something and the student doesn't get it," an elementary school student said, "don't just explain it again. Try to explain it in a different way." A middle school student wrote, "I'd have to make sure that this is what's going to help them learn better, since people learn differently."

A lack of patience made for unsuccessful teachers, they thought. A middle school student asked, "Why should you get mad at the person if they don't understand what you are trying to say and it doesn't get into their head?" They saw making mistakes as part of learning and believed that teachers needed to react to mistakes in a way that supported the students' effort to learn.

When I asked an elementary Learning Disabilities (LD) resource class what they would do if students made errors while learning, their reply was "Comfort them." One member of the class said that a student who thinks that he or she won't succeed at learning might turn into a "disbelieving person." Another added that, as a teacher, "You say, 'I'll help you.'"

Students understood that patience, practice, and expectations go together. A middle school student wrote about teaching a friend algebra: "I wouldn't let her quit until she had the right answer and knew how she'd gotten it." "You have to show them, then you have to tell them, and then you have to let them do it, and then you coach," wrote another middle school student. Being patient was connected with the belief that a student will eventually learn. A high school student stated, "Teachers are people who don't give up teaching."

Make Learning Fun

Making learning fun calls up the image of a work-free environment, but these students were not describing that kind of teaching. Probably the most careful statement of this idea came from a ninth grader: "I believe that if the information is presented in a fun and meaningful fashion to the student, then the student will grasp the information better. If the student believes that the information is significant and meaningful, then they will actually care about learning it. In my mind, that's what matters more than anything."

Their descriptions of fun involved hard work. A high school LD class said that learning should be both "fun and hard." Examples students gave of fun were rehearsals, team and dance practices, and other individual long-term work that developed into a product of which they were proud. Fun meant achievement—real achievement. A middle school student recalled a time when "I taught my class how to make beaded necklaces, bracelets, and earrings. It was a lot of fun, but it was also a lot of work."

Fun was pride in accomplishment. They described their pleasure in watching a younger sister or brother, or a friend showing off what they had learned. A high school student wrote:

I taught my little sister how to ride a bike. At first it was hard. She couldn't get what I was telling her. Then I held the bike while she rode it. I had to do that, otherwise she would fall down. So she began getting it. I was happier. She was starting to smile because she could ride like 30 feet and *then* fall down. After awhile she didn't fall. She was happy and OK.

To make learning fun was a conscious strategy related to the teacher's understanding of the student, as this middle school student explained:

First thing I would do when I'm just about to teach something is to ask the person some questions that would tell me more about the person and what he or she likes and dislikes. Then I would ask the person if he or she knew anything about the topic I am about to teach. Once I know how much the person knows about the subject, I would start teaching. I would take breaks every 20 minutes and joke around with the person, working with them along the way.

A high school student related her adventures teaching Spanish to her younger brother: "I make it fun and do stuff like insult my mom's friends who come over to dinner in Spanish so only my brother and I understand. He is enjoying learning now and is progressing nicely."

A seventh grader wrote about teaching a younger brother to hit in tee-ball. "It was the first day of my brother's tee-ball practice. As I watched him, I saw he knew which way to run and how to catch and throw." After this initial assessment, they spent hours practicing on a school playground as the older brother analyzed the younger brother's swing, stance, and concentration. Finally, he said, "After that (analysis and practice), his hitting improved a whole lot. I think my brother enjoyed my teaching him and I enjoyed it too. If there's anything else he needs help on, I'll enjoy helping him again." This feeling came after many hardworking sessions of instruction and practice and a sense of accomplishment for both teacher and student. It was fun.

Don't Be Boring

Not being boring meant, in general, a lack of rigidity and a respect for the learner. A teacher who was not being boring recognized important events and issues in students' lives, was able to change plans to acknowledge these events and issues, and was able to shift from assumptions they might have about students and to know when the situation called for it.

When teaching connected directly to students' lives, it wasn't boring. English Speakers of Other Languages (ESOL) students in an elementary school class said to start by teaching students to spell their names. One student told this story:

At the beginning of the year there was a new student. He did not know which bus number he was going on, so I told him it was #51 and he told his Mom. Then on the second day of school he did not have anyone to play with so I sat with him and then I was his friend. Then I told him some English. The first word I told him was my name.

Students will be bored if the learning offered is either something they already know or aren't ready to know. Not to be boring required the teacher's assessment of the students' learning needs and understanding of timing and readiness. A high school student told of teaching a fellow student using the concepts of assessment and readiness:

Once upon a time my friend needed help in Biology. I had already taken the course so I had a good grasp of the material. I knew he needed the help in Biology, but what? So I asked what he wanted to know, clarified it. Then he told me so I proceeded to explain something about chloroplasts. I asked if he understood but he was still a bit unclear on it, so I tried another way to communicate the idea to him and then he understood.

Not to be boring is also not to stereotype, not to cling to preconceived ideas. The students did not reject routines—they believed that practice was important—but they did not want to use rigid routines. A middle school student wrote, "Be open-minded, listen to students' suggestions. Don't be too stuck in a rut." They wanted to be able to change their teaching to fit their students.

TEACHING METHODS

The students knew that teaching takes skill beyond knowing the subject at hand. A middle school student wrote: "I feel that you need to be interested in what you are going to be teaching. Also the person needs to get interested. If the individual needs certain needs, know the needs and how to teach them." A high school student described a moment of understanding:

Yesterday my brother was having trouble understanding how to subtract. My mother was trying to explain but my brother still couldn't understand. I was doing my own homework. Then something clicked in my head. I had to think like a third grader!

The teaching methods the students recounted will sound familiar to teachers. They included modeling, starting at the beginning, making learning visual, questioning, evaluating, and rewarding.

Modeling and Demonstrating

The teaching method most frequently described was modeling and demonstrating the behavior to the person being taught. A first grader described teaching a younger brother: "I practice on doing it myself. I do it three times, then he does it." Another elementary school student laughed and related, "When I was spitting on my friend and sticking my tongue out at her and wobbling it, my little sister did it too, just like me." A high school student summed it up:

> I see myself as my little brother's teacher. He looks up to my older brother and me. If I do something, he is likely to do the same. I try making good examples, but they sometimes turn out bad. I try teaching him the right way. I guess I am influenced by my older brother. I want to do the same for my little brother.

Starting at the Beginning

They mentioned starting with what is fundamental to a task and then moving on to the more complicated part. "Don't let them get stuck," warned a middle school student. A high school student wrote: "In math everything sits on something else. Example: To divide you have to know how to multiply, so if you build on what you're trying to teach, it comes across better."

Making Learning Visual

They also mentioned using their hands and trying to make learning visual. A middle school student wrote: "One thing that helps me are my hands. I use them either to emphasize a point or to draw a picture in the person's mind." One student even used educational jargon: " I would make manipulatives so that they can visualize and work with what I am explaining to them."

Questioning

Asking questions was a frequent strategy. A middle school student said, "I would ask the person questions and see if they have any questions for me. This is the way I would teach."

Evaluating

They knew to check periodically to see if their students were learning. A second grader wrote:

> Once I told my brother not to stick his hand in the fence of our neighbors. Then I went home and peeked out the window to see if he was doing it. His friend came outside and stuck his hand in the fence. My brother said, "Don't stick your hand in the fence or the dog will bite you." I knew that he had listened.

Rewarding

And, finally, they sometimes used rewards as motivation. A middle school student said, "When he got it right, I gave him candy and that made him want to learn." Another advised: "Don't forget the final celebration!"

TEACHER AND STUDENT INTERACTION

The students recognized that teachers are learners. A high school student wanted to make his students "feel like they are not stupid, maybe tell them it took me awhile to learn also." An elementary school student recalled: "I taught M. karate. I taught him how to do a side kick, jump kick, and round kick. He taught K. all the things I taught him. He got better because he taught someone else."

They also described learning as interactive between teacher and student. A second grader described his teaching:

> I taught my brother not to use his hand when he is playing soccer. So I said, "Do not touch the ball or the person you are playing will get a penalty kick." And then I accidentally touched the ball. My brother said, "Do not touch the ball or the person will get a penalty."

They knew that even after students learn, a teacher's help might be needed. A middle school student wrote: "I taught my little brother how to put his spelling words in alphabetical order. And now he's like a pro at it, but sometimes he still needs help. I help him." On the other hand, students might surpass their teachers. A middle school student spoke of teaching his older brother how to improve his roller-skating. "So he kept pushing, gliding, and falling and eventually he became better than me."

LEARNING AND LIFE EXPERIENCE

Students saw learning as a natural result of life and teaching as a natural activity of human beings. An elementary school student wrote:

> I taught my mom about death and life. My mom's dad was in the hospital and she thought that he was going to die. I told her a phrase and it is: No matter if it is death or life, your father will be in your heart forever. My mom told me that I taught her something that she never knew.

A high school student made a similar statement:

> One time my friend was very sad because her grandmother was very close to dying. She was crying so when we got to math class I started talking to her and telling her my experiences with people dying in my family. When she heard about my family she felt a little better. If that's considered teaching.

The last line of the student's writing above stayed in my mind. "What *is* considered teaching?" Could school teachers teach as these students described? I tried comparing:

> The students often described teaching that took place away from school, or, if in school, as needed—a friend needs help with his math problems. Teacher researchers work in schools that decide how, when, and where teaching will take place and what is needed.
>
> The students usually described teaching as one on one. Teacher researchers teach in schools where one on one teaching is very rare; in fact, where they may have 30 or more students at a time.
>
> The students described teaching situations where they were free to invent teaching strategies, change their plans in response to student needs, and accept error as necessary to learning. Teacher researchers teach in schools where certain ways of teaching are prescribed, lesson plans, some prepackaged, are adhered to, and error translates as failure.
>
> The students taught because they wanted to and took pleasure in their students' learning. Teacher researchers teach in schools where pleasure is not a principle, where they often feel numbed by the tasks demanded of them.

These contrasts make the question, "What is teaching?" complicated at best. One student wrote, "Teaching and being a student are the only two things in life that whatever you put into, you get more out of than you put in." The chapters that follow are about those two valuable things in life and what teacher researchers and their students put into and get out of them.

REFERENCE

Lincoln, Y. (1995, April). *Emerging criteria for qualitative research*. Paper presented at the annual meeting of the American Educational Research Association, San Francisco.

CHAPTER 5

It All Adds Up: Learning Number Facts in First Grade

Betsy Sanford

I pretended it was 5 + 5 and then I knew it was 10, and then I put the two back on and that made 12.
—a first grader, explaining the solution to 7 + 5

Teaching first grade, I always found it exciting to watch my students develop as mathematicians, becoming more aware of mathematical ideas and relating them to their world. At the same time, however, I always worried about number fact recall. I puzzled over how recall of math facts fit into the bigger picture of conceptual understanding, wondered how to promote it, and worried about the time it took, when instructional time was always at such a premium.

For my first few years in first grade, I avoided teaching fact recall on its own. I knew that students needed rapid recall of addition and subtraction facts and I knew the basics about fact recall: that addition facts included the 100 problems ranging from 0 + 0 to 9 + 9; that there were only 55 facts once you accounted for duplicates (e.g., 4 + 3 and 3 + 4); that subtraction facts could be derived from addition facts; and that efficient recall meant recall in less than 3 seconds. What I didn't know was how to shape instruction in fact recall, and it was rarely the main objective of a math lesson. I hoped that I could model learning strategies for developing fact recall and then have students learn their facts at home.

Unfortunately, this instructional plan didn't work. I had to admit that my students just didn't have the basic facts at their fingertips. That is why the focus of my classroom research became, "How do first graders learn number facts?"

DATA COLLECTION

The data I collected during this research project includes timed fact tests, worksheets, and homework assignments done by students. I also observed and videotaped students working on math facts and conducted group and individual student interviews. I kept a research log to reflect on and write about class lessons and activities. I also kept anecdotal records to document my students' math thinking. Finally, my lesson plans yielded data about my instructional decisions, helping me trace shifts in my thinking as I conducted this research.

GETTING STARTED ON NUMBER FACTS

It was late November, and we had been working on addition for several weeks. I noticed that students still didn't seem familiar with many of the basic facts, in spite of encountering them repeatedly. I had some hunches about my students' knowledge of basic facts, but I realized I wasn't certain what they knew or how they knew it. I decided to look more closely by timing each student on an addition facts test.

Since I believed that timed tests produce anxiety and that speed of recall doesn't necessarily correlate with math understanding, I was a little surprised I decided on this course. However, a timed test could tell me exactly what I wanted to know: How fast could my students recall answers to simple addition facts? One morning I made up a sheet of 24 addition facts (using addends no higher than 6) and administered it to three students at a time.

The timed test confirmed what I had expected, that although students understood addition, they had very few fact answers at their fingertips. At that point I resolved to remedy the situation; I would find ways to help my students develop rapid recall of all the addition number facts.

Over the next few weeks I planned classwork and homework activities focused on learning facts. I started doing daily oral drills, first with doubles facts (e.g., 3 + 3) and later with other facts, including the combinations-for-ten and the plus-one and plus-two facts. Students loved these drills. As one student said later, "[Until then], I never knew how it felt knowing math so fast." I was temporarily satisfied.

In early January I timed my students again and found that most had improved their accuracy and speed of recall. Wanting to know more, I analyzed which facts students had missed on the November and January tests. I wrote in my research log:

So what does all this tell me? Well, only a couple of things, I think. The first is that (of these facts) the single fact, 6 + 4, is the most difficult for kids. . . . And, of course, the "six" facts are the toughest of all. Does that have any implications for instruction? Or, rather, what *are* the implications for instruction?

> I feel that there are two approaches here. The first is simple drill
> on the "six" facts. The second is giving kids a *way* to *think* about
> 6 (or even, maybe, a way to *see* 6) for instance with the tens frame.
> It seems to me that if they have a sense of 6 in relationship to 10
> and 5, they might do better.

That entry marked a turning point in my thinking about number fact
learning. Considering what learning particular "six" facts might involve, I
started wondering what might be true about learning other sets of facts.
For instance, 6 + 4 was an easy fact if one saw its relationship to 5 + 5, but
it was clear my students did not make that connection. I needed to know
more.

At this point, I might have saved myself time and worry if I had made a
connection to research on using a strategic approach to learning number
facts. A strategic approach involves learning to recognize number facts by
the characteristics which will make solving them efficient. Van de Walle
(2004) divides addition facts into these categories: one- or two-more than
facts (3 + 1, 2 + 6); zero facts (0 + 8); doubles facts (4 + 4); near-doubles
facts (4 + 5); and make-ten facts (8 + 3, 4 + 9). According to Van de Walle
and others, addition facts include addends no higher than 9, but throughout
my research I included problems with 10 as an addend and referred to them
as facts. I also included combinations-for-ten as a separate fact category.

Regarding the fact categories, much research confirms that doubles
require memorization but are very easily learned. Combinations-for-ten
also require memorization and are more challenging for students to recall,
but they are one of the most useful number relationship tools for numerical reasoning, making learning them well worth a student's time and effort.
Answers for facts in the other categories can be derived by using number
relationships. The number fact 7 + 2 provides an example. Students can
find an addition answer by "counting on"—in this case, starting with 7 and
counting on two more. However, students working efficiently will use their
conceptual knowledge about the two-more-than/two-less-than relationship
between 7 and 9 and quickly see that the answer is 9.

Separating addition facts into the categories specified by Van de Walle
and including the combinations-for-ten as an additional category, we are
left with only four "difficult" facts to memorize (5 + 3, 6 + 3, 7 + 4, and 7
+ 5)—a much less daunting task than memorizing as many as 55 facts!

Although I was familiar with fact classification, I thought that it was
simply a management system for drill. I had not yet made a connection
between fact categorization and the data from my students. The two sets of
timed tests were evidence that specific facts (for instance, 6 + 4) might be
easy or difficult, but I was just beginning to consider why that might be.

I was curious but unsure about what to do next and decided I might learn more by testing my students on the full range of addition facts for sums to 12. This time I decided to test students individually and planned to note four behaviors I might observe: (a) immediate recall, (b) recall after some hesitation, (c) use of fingers to solve a problem, and (d) counting on (e.g., for 3 + 7, saying "7, 8, 9, 10"). I was particularly interested in counting on because, like using fingers, it is procedural rather than conceptual. Both methods give students a way to get an answer but discourage them from using number relationships to solve the problem efficiently.

The first students I tested were Ray and Mary. I recorded Ray's time and wrote "never used his fingers," evidence that suggested he had excellent fact recall or, when he didn't, was able to think conceptually about the numbers he was adding. Watching Mary was more revealing. She knew many facts instantly, but whenever she didn't, she resorted to counting on. For example, when she worked 4 + 7, she lightly tapped her pencil four times next to the 4 and then wrote the answer. After the test was finished, I asked Mary about her pencil tapping. She explained that it was her way to quickly get answers when she did worksheets at home with her father.

My experience with these two students told me how much I could learn by just watching. Observing my third student, Valerie, and looking over her paper afterwards, I saw that she had done every double, plus-zero, and plus-one fact quickly. The turning point for her was the plus-two facts, where she had done 4 of the 10 problems quickly. Of the remaining 14 difficult facts, she had answered only 2 quickly. Looking for a way to encourage her to keep working on her facts, I told her I could see she was making progress and suggested, "Ask your mom to just work on the plus-two facts with you."

Analyzing Valerie's performance was a catalyst for rethinking my assumptions. I had assumed that if students could do plus-one facts, they would also know how to think about plus-two and plus-three facts. Valerie's work challenged that assumption—plus-two facts were much more difficult than plus-one facts for her, and plus-three facts were harder still. That information pushed me to consider the important link between fact categories and number relationship concepts. Finally I grasped that categories were not simply a way to manage fact drill, but were a blueprint for instruction, helping me determine the number concepts and number relationships that students needed in order to master number fact recall.

WHAT I LEARNED

I continued my one-on-one testing of students over the next several days. Sometimes I had students identify a number fact that was difficult or asked them how they had solved a particular problem. Their answers revealed a range of ways that they thought about number facts and found solutions.

- Bridget said, in discussing 5 + 6, "I knew what 6 + 6 was and I just took one away."
- Carl replied, when asked about 6 + 4, "I just knew it. I've done that problem lots of times."
- Carol, reporting on 2 + 7, said, "I did the high number and then did the 2."
- Yuta told how he solved 7 + 5: "I pretended it was 5 + 5 and then I knew it was 10, and then I put two back on and that made 12."

As I rethought number fact learning over the next several weeks, I experimented with new teaching strategies and materials and also returned to familiar ones, but with new purposes. At each step I used what students said and did to help decide how to proceed. Gradually, a new understanding of how first graders learn number facts emerged for me. My research influenced my thinking in six areas of number fact learning: using fact categories, working procedurally and strategically, developing number relationships, varying ways to practice, giving students choice, and educating parents.

Using Fact Categories

My first decision was to work on facts by category. I saw this as a process with two intertwined but distinct steps. First, students had to be familiar with the categories and develop a vocabulary with which to talk about them. At the same time, though, students had to learn to classify facts in terms of those categories. Students had been used to seeing addition facts as two numbers to put together. Now the emphasis was on searching for number relationships—realizing, for instance, that 6 + 5 was a near-double, not just that it was 6 plus five more.

I chose activities to help students practice generalizing about facts. For instance, students might go through a set of flash cards and find the near-doubles or plus-two facts, or their ticket to lunch might be to say a combination-for-ten. I concentrated on parallel goals: providing practice with particular facts and helping students think about facts in terms of their classifications.

Working Procedurally, Working Strategically

Working with students on number facts, I thought again about the distinction between procedural knowledge and conceptual knowledge.

Procedural knowledge involves knowing how to do something—for instance, knowing how to do the "crossouts" of subtraction regrouping (e.g., 74 becomes $^{6}\cancel{7}\,^{1}4$). That is procedural knowledge. Conceptual knowledge, on the other hand, involves understanding why the crossouts work: understanding that this notation represents renaming 74 as 60 and 14. Procedural and conceptual knowledge are different ways of knowing and can operate independently of each other.

I often see first graders who have the procedural knowledge to perform a task but have not mastered the conceptual knowledge related to the task. The dissonance becomes obvious when they must apply their knowledge in a new setting. One example is "skip counting;" many first graders learn to skip count by fives. It's tempting to assume that they have mastered the underlying concept, but sometimes it only appears that way. For instance, students might confidently count by fives to calculate the value of a group of nickels. However, when pennies are added to the nickels, even though students know a penny's value, they often count both the nickels and the pennies by fives. Thus, four nickels and three pennies would be counted "5, 10, 15, 20, 25, 30, 35." Those students are relying on procedural knowledge but have not demonstrated conceptual knowledge related to skip counting.

As I worked with my students on number facts, I was again struck by the importance of distinguishing between conceptual and procedural knowledge. It was clear that some students knew how to get answers but did not consistently use number relationships. The explanations of two students who solved 7 + 5 on the second timed test reveal different kinds of knowing. The first student's "I knew it was like 6 + 6" shows strategic thinking and a reliance on conceptual knowledge by using the relationships among 5, 6, and 7 to get the answer. On the other hand, the second student's explanation, "I started with the 7 and then counted 8, 9, 10, 11, 12," shows a procedural approach.

I believed that if students talked about how they solved fact problems, they might become more aware of the strategies available to them. Often our discussions produced several ways to solve a fact. These discussions allowed students to notice, articulate, value, and integrate the thinking their peers and they had done.

Asking students to share their thinking had the advantage of letting me see when students were working procedurally or strategically. Often students' comments suggested ways that I could intervene. I encouraged them to think about what they knew about a number in order to find connections that might help them solve the problem at hand. Listening to them reinforced my belief about how important it was that they learn to look for the solution possibilities.

Developing Number Concepts and Number Relationships

I was still curious about what else I might do and realized that students who could see possibilities were students who could think flexibly about numbers. To do that, one must have a sound foundation in number concepts and number relationships. Students must be able to take numbers apart and put them back together in a variety of ways.

I realized my students needed more work on number relationships, and particularly on the one-more-than/one-less-than, and two-more-than/two-less-than relationships, as well as on how numbers relate to the anchor numbers of 5 and 10. We had often worked on number relationships with materials such as dot cards, tens frames cards, domino cards, and hidden number cards. (See the chapter appendix for further information.) I returned to those materials, now asking students to point out connections that might help them solve a number fact. Students began to see, for instance, that the configuration for 7 on a tens frame card could help them solve 5 + 2 or 7 + 3. I put even greater stress on knowing the combinations-for-ten. I reasoned that familiarity with ways to make ten would give students another path for solving many number fact problems (e.g., by relating 7 + 4 to 6 + 4).

Using a Variety of Ways to Practice

When I recalled Mary's reliance on counting on and thought about the worksheets she did so often at home, I began to rethink pencil-and-paper drill. I suspected that if Mary had been practicing facts in a variety of ways she might have developed more strategies for recall. As it was, counting on met her needs—it allowed her to complete her drill sheets fairly quickly. However, Mary's performance told me that too much emphasis on written drill could put students on automatic pilot and keep them from making connections and noticing number relationships as they solved problems.

Because of this, I began to use more fact recall games and activities. I also began relying more on oral drill, fitting it in whenever we had a spare moments. One day, I might concentrate on the combinations-for-ten, another day, I might ask students for near-doubles. These oral drills were quick and gave students practice with number relationships and practice in thinking by category.

Giving Students Choice

As could be expected, students mastered categories at different rates. For instance, most students took a long time to develop a strategy for solving near-doubles, but a few did it quickly. Because students were working on different groups of facts, I knew that their work had to be individualized. Students needed to know which facts they should work on, and they needed the opportunity to work on just those facts. This meant that I had to select materials and activities that could be tailored to individual needs, so that both at school and at home students could concentrate on just the facts they needed to practice.

Educating Parents and Enlisting Their Help

The individual nature of number fact learning told me that parents needed to play a key role. However, most parents were not familiar with a strategic approach to learning number facts. I used parent meetings, the weekly newsletter, and school and homework assignments to communicate to parents how they could use fact categories and emphasize number relationships as they worked with their children on fact recall.

A CENTRAL FINDING:
NUMBER FACTS AND PROBLEM SOLVING

As I continued my research, a list of tentative findings about number fact learning emerged. For instance, I knew students could learn to see facts in categories, and I knew they found some categories easy and some hard. Then, preparing a presentation to share my research with other teachers, I made one more connection.

The previous year I had attended a conference on problem solving sponsored by my school district. The keynote speaker, Sid Rachlin (University of North Carolina), had talked about solving problems in terms of three key behaviors: generalizability, flexibility, and reversibility.

Now I saw a connection between those three key problem-solving behaviors and my number fact mastery. When students tried to link facts to categories, they had to generalize about the fact and see it as part of a larger group. And in order to choose efficiently among categories, students had to think flexibly about the numbers involved. As students did this mental work of looking for relationships and thinking flexibly about numbers, they worked forwards and backwards, negotiating between categories and number relationships. It was then that I realized that when students moved beyond rote memory and procedure in fact learning, they were problem solving.

Seeing number fact learning from a problem-solving perspective helped me appreciate its real value in the first grade curriculum. I finally understood that this work goes to the heart of conceptual understanding. It requires students to use number sense, number concepts, and number relationships in order to gain control of the numbers they are working with. That, in turn, helped me see the importance of using class time to develop number fact recall. Believing now that students' speed of recall is intimately tied to their development of number concepts and number relationships, I see the time we spend on math facts as rich with mathematical content.

A QUESTION FOR FURTHER STUDY

Although my number fact research answered a lot of my questions, it raised the question of mental math and the influence a strategic approach to number facts in the early grades might have on the development of numerical reasoning. What would happen, I wondered, to primary students who have learned to move beyond using only written algorithms and procedures? Will first graders who are encouraged to look for a way to solve 7 + 5, instead of simply memorizing 7 + 5 = 12, become fourth graders who feel confident solving problems like 149 + 256 using mental math and a problem-solving approach? What would the instructional program look like that would help students become those confident mathematicians?

Since the time of this number fact research I have become a mathematics resource teacher in the same elementary school. Working with students from kindergarten through sixth grade, I have been made keenly aware of the importance of a rich foundation in numerical reasoning and fluency. Such an approach can, I believe, start with our youngest students when we emphasize number relationships and a strategic approach to number fact learning. While there are more questions to answer, these goals for our students are unimpeachable, and since we know how to start students on this path, we must begin. It's important work, it's exciting, and—we should remember—it all adds up!

APPENDIX

There are three materials—dot cards, tens frames, and hidden number cards—that are especially helpful as students work to develop number sense, number concepts, and number relationships. Both dot cards and hidden number cards are used by many math educators and, to my knowledge, no particular person is given credit for their creation. Van de Walle (2004) credits Robert Wirtz with the development of the tens frame, although his own work with the tens frame has brought it to the attention of many teachers.

The chapter "The Development of Number Concepts and Number Sense," in Van de Walle's book is a helpful reference for the use of these materials.

Dot Cards

Dot cards use configurations similar to those on dice to represent the numbers 1 through 10. For example, two common configurations for the number 10 are the "eggcrate" five-and-five design and the "bowling pin triangle" of one, two, three and four dots. Dot cards help students develop number sense and number relationships by reinforcing a sense of the relative magnitude of numbers and by providing visual ways to think about numbers in relationship to each other.

Tens Frames Cards

Tens frames cards are similar to dot cards but are more advanced because they illustrate a number's relationship to 5 and 10. Here are two examples of tens frames cards:

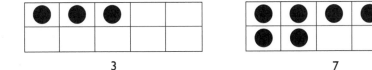

3   7

Hidden Number Cards

Hidden number cards are designed to present a number broken into two parts. Each card has two flaps: students see the numeral for the number represented on the card and, when the first flap is opened, they see both the numeral and the dot representation for one part of the number. The numeral and dot representation for the other part of the number are under the other flap. Hidden number cards look like this:

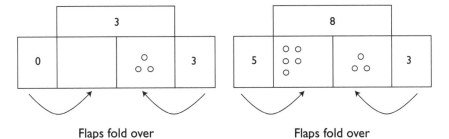

Flaps fold over   Flaps fold over

Along with hidden number cards, I also use "the hiding game," based on Richardson's (1999) hiding assessment. Working with an individual student, I put four, five, or six small objects in my hand and have the student count them. Then I hide some in one hand and show the student the rest, asking how many are hidden. Initially, the hiding game and hidden number cards are difficult for students. Soon, however, they become adept at both activities and enjoy playing the game and making their own hidden number cards to use with their classmates and family.

REFERENCES

Richardson, K. (1999). *Developing number concepts using unifix cubes*. White Plains, NY: Dale Seymour.

Van de Walle, J. (2004). *Elementary and middle school mathematics: Teaching developmentally* (5th ed.). Boston: Allyn & Bacon.

CHAPTER 6

Paying Attention in a Different Way: How Teacher Researchers Teach

Marian M. Mohr

Teacher research is paying attention in a different way.
—a member of a teacher research group

This chapter explores the question, How do teacher researchers teach? Narratives of teaching and learning in teacher researchers' classrooms and discussions of those narratives alternate with explanations of the research process used to interpret the narratives. I chose this organization of my research experience because my developing understanding of both data and process was interactive as well as cumulative.

The first narrative, "Chemistry Review," takes place during a class review of the chemical unit, moles. The teacher researcher is revising her way of teaching through her research. She is paying attention in a different way, as am I, an observer in her classroom.

NARRATIVE: CHEMISTRY REVIEW

The room is dim, and the lesson is a review of moles based on data from a videotape, past laboratory experiments, and information from the text. The students, each with a review worksheet/study guide with space for writing, sit at tables with their learning groups. I sit with one of the groups.

The teacher is investigating how students learn in cooperative groups in a chemistry class. She is also interested in changes to her way of approaching students. She states this question as "How am I to change my role in the classroom from that of a director (or dictator) to that of an observer, encourager, and supporter?"

Today she wants the class to connect the information on the video to what they have been learning experimentally and from their text, writing on the worksheet as they see the connections. She stops the videotape from time to time and checks to see how they are doing. She questions the videotape, the information on their study guide, and the students themselves, all the while using short encouraging phrases such as "Use your knowledge" and "Listen carefully, this is interesting!"

The students alternately view, write, and question, sometimes clarifying an answer with each other. The teacher continues to move among them, inquiring, approving, and suggesting. At what used to be the front of the room, the lectern stands untouched.

When the teacher and I reflect afterwards, I tell her that I counted at least seven different ways of learning that she offered her students in this one lesson. She adds a few more to my list and remarks that it is because of the cooperative learning groups that she is able to offer such a variety, and she thinks that her students are learning more as a result of the different approaches.

Narrative Discussion: Chemistry Review

Her enthusiasm for chemistry and her well-planned yet flexible lesson were signs of any good teacher. What of her teaching could be called teacher research? First of all, she had begun the year with a research question, What happens when I teach chemistry with heterogeneous learning groups? That question had led her toward a second, How can I become a more encouraging supportive teacher? Her questions were generated from her interest in her students' learning and connected to both teaching content and classroom management.

Examining data from the learning groups led her to develop ways of learning other than the lecture note-taking procedure she was used to—students talking to each other, writing, asking questions, creating their own review sheet, and comparing visual, written, and experimental data. By constantly comparing new data with old in her research group, she developed new understandings of how her students learned, and, also with the support of her research group, she developed and tried out new ways of teaching. She directed her own professional development.

Research Process: Questions and Data

My notes from the observation with the chemistry teacher researcher were data to help me answer my own research questions: Does teaching by teacher researchers have distinctive characteristics? Do students notice these characteristics? If so, how do they understand and react to them? What are the meaningful connections between teaching as a researcher and the ways of learning in a classroom? How do teacher researchers teach?

The one certainty in my research plan was to collect data from time spent with teacher researchers and their students. Eventually, my data would consist of observations in teacher researchers' classrooms over 3 years on 82 different occasions with the three teacher researcher leaders and 31 other members of the research groups. I divided my time among elementary, middle, and high schools and among classrooms of various disciplines—mathematics, English, social studies, science. I worked with students from a wide variety of social and cultural backgrounds, for many of whom English was a second language.

The teachers' experience varied from 1 to over 20 years. The teacher researcher leaders—Marion MacLean, Betsy Sanford, and Sheila Clawson, referred to by name—had completed several research projects over the past 14 years and had published in professional journals. Most of the other teacher researchers in the school groups, referred to by their subjects and grade levels, were conducting research for the first time, as was the case with the science teacher in the narrative "Chemistry Review." The next narrative takes place in Betsy Sanford's first-grade classroom. Sanford is both an experienced teacher and researcher.

NARRATIVE: SOLVING PROBLEMS

Before the students arrive, Betsy Sanford is busy at her computer. Her computer-written plans read like a combination of journal entries (questions, reflections, and memoranda) and schedules (long-range goals for the class and individual projects for particular students). She describes the lesson structure as one "that kids work from, not that kids duplicate."

For some time her research has been on mathematics learning. Today the first graders are seated on the rug in front of the chalkboard. She writes a problem on the board and reads it aloud.

Patti lost 3 marbles.
Now she only has 6 marbles.
How many marbles did she have before?

They stop to make sure everyone in the multilingual class understands the English word *marble*. Sanford then instructs the students to go to their desks and write the problem with the answer as soon as they figure out how to solve it. When they come back to the rug, they will each explain how they figured it out.

Gradually the students begin to move toward their desks, some asking questions of Sanford before they go. A few stay longer, talking the problem over until they think they've got it. One works at the chalkboard, using lines to represent the marbles in the problem.

When all are gathered on the rug again, they take turns explaining how they figured out the answer. One student says, "She had to have *more* before." The student at the board turns around and says to the class, "I thought I didn't know it. Then I thought, 'No, now I understand.'"

Sanford makes her own questioning behavior explicit to her students. Once she stopped in the middle of a lesson to say, "I am just trying to figure this out. I think I did it wrong in my planning."

On another day when the class is reviewing math facts using pink dot flash cards, Sanford says proudly, "You guys know your doubles!" The children discuss the thinking that enables them to get the answers. One student concludes, "If you have to add two numbers, it's faster if you start with the larger number and add on the smaller."

They also discuss thinking as a way to solve math problems. A student turns to me, points to the wall, and says, "Up there it says 'Math is for our minds.' I have to do that [thinking] all the time!" Another student adds, "You keep on thinking when you're trying to figure things out. Other people will wait for you while you are thinking."

Later in the year, Sanford tells the students that she wants them to try a problem again that they had a hard time with earlier. She says she thinks they can do it now. She writes on the board the following:

The problem is to draw a design or picture, using at least two different shapes as many times as necessary, to add up to 15.

They rush to tell her their problem-solving ideas. One says, "I know a way to do it!" They discuss their theories of problem solving with each other as they go to their desks. Some create elaborate drawings with houses and trees added; others make direct representations of the geometric shapes. They compare their drawings and their problem-solving strategies, exclaiming over the differences. Sanford explains to me that she based her lesson on her developing findings and theories about learning math facts.

Narrative Discussion: Solving Problems

Characteristics of teacher researcher teaching in this narrative included emphasis on how the students learn as well as what they learn, encouragement of the students to develop new strategies for learning and to share them with each other, and stepping back to let students take the lead in discussions.

Sanford's planning was focused on both specific students and goals for the whole class, flexible enough to take advantage of learning opportunities and needs. She accepted and valued her students' contributions to her research, and they knew their participation was important. Sanford's teaching and research were integrated, so much so that her students were used to her stopping to record something that happened in their learning.

They and she saw their earlier difficulty with a problem as information, something for which they now have more problem-solving skills. The students solved math problems and helped their teacher learn about how math problems are solved by them.

Research Process: Planning to Observe

I was excited to be a participant and observer in classrooms like Sanford's and the high school chemistry teacher's. Because I began observing in other teacher researchers' classrooms soon after I retired from high school teaching, I hoped my experience as a teacher researcher would help me understand the teaching and learning in their classrooms. But I was also wary of my role and my perceptions. I had mistrusted outside observers who summarized my teaching in superficial checklists and overgeneralized phrases. Would I turn into one of them? Or, the opposite, would I be unable to maintain a researcher stance and find myself intervening and assuming?

I hoped that my plans to write and reflect with the teacher researchers as part of my research process would help me balance my current position as an outsider with my past as an insider and teaching colleague. Their suggestions and my increasing experience in others' classrooms led to the development of the criteria I would use for observing and writing up observations:

- Participating as both a teacher and a researcher, making my research motives transparent
- Writing in response to my own observations and those of the teacher and the students
- Coordinating the written accounts of observations with the teacher researchers as equal partners
- Creating trust by listening and being a responsible, active contributor to classroom activities and research group meetings
- Classifying my notes to include actions and theories of both teachers and students as well as questions from us all

- Reflecting, usually on the same day, with the teacher researchers about their intentions, the classroom context, and how they viewed what had happened

I was prepared for the complexity of even a brief classroom observation. The thickest description seems thin in comparison to what actually happens. But as a researcher, I had to make choices, to uncover and describe essentials. In the next narrative, set in a middle school undergoing renovation, the complexity of the competing demands on teachers and students was evident.

NARRATIVE: FINDING OUT TO FIND OUT

It is second period, creative writing. Sheila Clawson, the teacher researcher, has been away at a professional conference for a few days. She listens to reports about the substitute while she pushes two computer stations down the hall from her first-period classroom. A student calls after her, "Have you got everything, Mrs. Clawson?" The students themselves are laden with their writing portfolios.

She begins class by reviewing the elements of short stories that they had been discussing before she left. She also reminds them of what they are learning in English about fables. She asks, "Did you read the slug descriptions I left for you while I was gone?"

"Yes!"

"Gross!"

She smiles. All the students have their portfolios and are assigned to computers. It's Thursday, and a story draft is due on Monday.

The students begin to write as Clawson moves around the room answering questions. She believes that writing on computers is important, and the students regularly see her composing on hers. She has managed to borrow enough computers so that students only have to share with one other person.

Two students sit close together hovering over the computer. They speak Vietnamese to each other and pass the mouse back and forth as they compose a story about their family in English. They are new arrivals to the school and have been placed in creative writing to help them get more practice writing.

At one point the class is very quiet except for the sound of the computers. Clawson leans against a table and looks over the class. In a few minutes they must pack up again and return the computers to their original classrooms. Her next class is in yet another room.

For a number of years Clawson has conducted classroom research on learning in small groups. She says she adapts what she learns from researchers outside the classroom to what she observes inside it. This year she is developing strategies with her English students to evaluate their own group work.

Her English class is working on their "museums," the finale of a year-long research project combining several disciplines of the middle school team. Materials—paper, fabric, scissors, and so on—are in use around the room. Clawson speaks with individuals, with groups, and with the whole class, shifting among them, asking and answering questions, occasionally stopping to jot something down.

One student comes to her and complains, "I'm so mad. None of my group is doing anything."

"If you feel like they're not doing their part, you need to talk to them about it. Have you done that?" Clawson replies. The student goes back to the group and presents his case.

Another group is planning a hurricane as part of their exhibit on natural disasters. Strips of black paper go up on the walls, as well as blue velvet. As they work, they discuss the issue of how topics and displays in a museum should relate to each other.

Although teacher research helps her "make professional, informed decisions" in her teaching, Clawson regards it as more than staff development to promote changes in teaching. "You find out to find out! That's a result! Even if I change something in one class and generalize across my classes, it doesn't necessarily turn out the same. Something seems simple, and you say, 'I'll change this,' but it turns out to be very complicated."

Narrative Discussion: Finding Out to Find Out

As a teacher researcher, Clawson observed her students closely. She helped them take more responsibility for their own learning while at the same time acknowledging their level of maturity. (I once saw her pull out three brightly colored scarves and teach the class to juggle during a few minutes of downtime created by an administrative mix-up.) In addition to observing her students, Clawson responded carefully to their suggestions and included their ideas in her teaching, as she did with the evaluation criteria for group learning.

She intended to be a model of inquiry in her classroom. I asked her how it matters that her students have a teacher researcher for a teacher. "They're privileged to know. I'm modeling for them what I want them to do, to be reflective, to stop and think about what's going on." They became learning partners with her.

Clawson had professional responsibilities and opportunities outside the school. She said, "When I'm gone from the school building—to a conference or a meeting—I lose time at school that I need, planning for classes and doing my research." She added, "Of course, it's a perception of teachers that they need to be here in school." She placed a high value on both her time with her students and her professional time with colleagues, but the two often seemed incompatible.

Because of her reduced teaching load as a result of the grant funding, she did not have a classroom of her own nor was she able to function as a member of a middle school team. Conflicting choices in their professional lives were often a problem for teacher researchers.

Research Process: Data Analysis

As the Clawson narrative shows, I learned how closely teacher researchers' professional lives were connected to the way they taught. I also began to recognize some similarities in their teaching. I started a list of these characteristics, such as modeling the behavior of a learner that the chemistry teacher, Sanford, and Clawson all exemplified. I added any connections I could see between teaching and learning in their classrooms. I carried the list to every observation and every meeting of teacher researchers I attended, adding and revising it in response to suggestions from other teacher researchers. My own rethinking and reseeing of the data over time caused additional revisions.

Observing in three schools at various grade levels and with teacher researchers of differing experience levels helped me focus on those distinctive characteristics that appeared in all the classrooms. I trusted the knowledge of my teacher researcher colleagues and they patiently described and clarified their work while helping me move in and out of their classrooms with increasing familiarity. In the next narrative, a high school math teacher gives advice to his students, which also proved helpful to my analysis: "Think of as many ways to analyze as possible."

NARRATIVE: MATH PROJECTS

These 11th-grade students have just received an assignment sheet entitled "Project 2: Cubic Equations." The project, says the paper, will help them "develop a complete understanding of the cubic equation" and "explore the techniques of math analysis."

This is the second time their teacher has assigned projects, and although he is studying the use of graphing calculators as his research this year, he already knows he wants to study the projects next. He has also encouraged his students to write their own brief "textbooks" on various kinds of problem-solving techniques. He considers their assigned textbook confusing and not well written.

The assignment sheet includes 10 project questions and 3 extension questions that go "above and beyond." One project question asks:

> How can graphing help you find solutions to a cubic equation?
> Does every cubic equation have at least one real solution?

Today the teacher plans for the students to use the period to work on their projects. Before they begin, they are turning in their worksheets from yesterday's lab and asking last-minute questions. When the questions have ended, the students begin to move about in the room. The teacher reminds them, "Think of as many ways to analyze as possible."

The student sitting next to me explains the relationship between the projects and the test that follows. She says, "The projects are about questions and problem solving, the test is about right answers. You use the project and the project notes to study for the test."

I ask, "Does doing the project teach you to solve the problems on the test?"

"Yes, you need to have different ways to analyze for the problems on the test."

The teacher walks among the students as they work, answering individual questions, prodding, speaking about individual issues, and giving reminders.

After class, he says with some frustration, "They don't all take advantage of project days, but I realized that I needed some days when I don't lecture. They work on their projects, ask questions. Then I tell them a lecture is coming up, and they have a reason to listen."

Sometimes he leaves something out of a lecture on purpose, saying to the class, "I couldn't figure out how to do this." Once when he "couldn't figure out" something, a student created a strategy for solving the problem. He asked her to share the strategy with the rest of the class, and then added it to his lecture, giving her credit, in his next class.

Narrative Discussion: Math Projects

The teacher indicated to his students that there were different ways to learn and that they had valuable contributions to make to the learning in the classroom. The students knew that he used their contributions to help them all learn. His current research question was leading him to teach differently and to have a different relationship with his students.

His work on graphing calculators was connected to their being introduced into high school mathematics classrooms. He wanted to find out how they work best in his teaching and his colleagues in the department wanted to know what he would find out.

Research Process: Narrative as Research

When we worked to arrange the math projects narrative in a way that the teacher and I thought was true to what had happened, we knew that we were not working in a white-gloved experimental research tradition. In fact, however, I had clung to listing findings and arranging data as tightly focused vignettes or objective-sounding reports because I didn't want to tell stories. I had often heard stories dismissed as "anecdotal" and had listened to university researchers explain that stories are not rigorous, not research.

As I struggled with ways to present the data, I turned to a relatively new book on my shelf, *Narrative Inquiry* (2000) by D. Jean Clandinin and F. Michael Connelly. As usual with books addressed to qualitative researchers, I needed to make adaptations to see teacher research in their descriptions, but they suggested a way I could position the observation data ("field texts") in three dimensions—time, place, and personal-social (p. 117). These are dimensions of the context of the classroom observations, and they were usable guidelines for me in turning the data into narratives.

Patricia Stock's *The Dialogic Curriculum* (1995) was the next reference I sought. She writes directly about teacher research—her own—and discusses narrative as needing to be shaped out of "raw data" (p. 98). Although my observation notes were raw data, I had forgotten the many times I had told the stories of the observations to my colleagues as Stock did. Through those retellings and the resulting revisions, I was working my way toward the larger narratives told about teaching in general. I realized that I could shape both the findings and the data toward that end.

Finally, just in time, Bob Fecho's (2003) talk about writing and publishing teacher research appeared in *Research in the Teaching of English*. I too wanted to write in a way that was acceptable to both my colleagues and to academics. I needed his reminder of the importance of my own presence in my research and of the story of my question, its history in my life (p. 289). Close to that history is my colleague, Marion MacLean, the teacher researcher of the next narrative.

NARRATIVE: TEACHING AS RESEARCH

The room is hung with large sheets of newsprint—hand-written assignments. Also posted are notes from class discussions and parts of other lessons such as term definitions. The newsprint shows various changes, updates, and student handwriting as well as the teacher's.

It's first period; school business comes first: Homecoming Queen vote today, candidate forum tomorrow. The students, 12th graders, are looking through "blurt" drafts—written quickly, not revised or edited—and following directions to find and mark vivid passages. The drafts are part of their preparation for writing an essay about themselves suitable for a college entrance application. Marion MacLean, their English teacher, gives written and oral directions, but she also walks through the class and responds directly to individual students, having brief conversations with nearly every one.

They discuss what *vivid* means. One student says, "*Vivid* means not too clear, right?"

MacLean answers, "Actually it means *very* clear—alive."

Another student adds, "As in, Vive la France!"

MacLean asks, "What is the word in Spanish?"

A student responds with a smile, "Viva!" They begin to shuffle through their papers and mark them, also filling in answers to MacLean's questions on the assignment sheet.

Near the end of the class, she asks, "Help me understand what you've done."

"I marked what were important events in my life."

"All my writings were strange."

"The topics have all changed since I first wrote about them."

MacLean takes notes on what they say in her composition book/research log. Later she will examine her log writing and their responses on the assignment sheet to see what they understood from the lesson. She does part of her planning in that same research log.

In another class, labeled "gifted and talented," her 10th-grade students are beginning *The Merchant of Venice* while finishing up a unit on poetry. For homework, the students have written definitions of *justice* and *mercy*, and now, in small groups, they read them to each other. The room is full of animated talking, students holding papers in their hands and referring to them as they talk. They have been asked to choose definitions from their group to be read to the whole class.

MacLean gets her research log, sits on a stool in front of the class, and writes as they begin to read aloud. They will listen to all the definitions before they talk. When the reading concludes, the discussion breaks out.

"Could mercy have a bad effect?"

"Punishment is for prevention. It doesn't necessarily give justice. You can't bring back the dead."

"Mercy is meant to stop future suffering. Justice is to make sure everyone gets the same amount of suffering."

Just before class is over, MacLean asks them to write at the bottom of their definition sheet any comments they didn't get to make during the discussion. They write quickly and with concentration, as if determined to have their say, and hand them in.

MacLean is conducting her "real" research in her 12th-grade classes on what they see as reasons for studying literature, but she collects data routinely in all her classes. "I know to collect things. They might be useful— research questions change." She keeps her research log open and takes notes off and on throughout every class.

Narrative Discussion: Teaching as Research

MacLean's assignment sheets, her homework assignments, even the walls of the classroom were part of her research process, providing documentation of how her students were learning. At one discussion after an observation, I asked MacLean which of her actions she would identify as those of a teacher researcher. She didn't name a specific action. Research, she said, helps her learn what she doesn't know. She gets information from her students. "They evaluate their own learning, make choices, and try out different learning strategies."

The seniors had chosen to read *Hamlet*, and she had responded to their concerns about how difficult it would be to read by working out a series of strategies they would use as they read the play, leading toward live production of the final scenes. "Students become more reflective and responsible when they see their contributions to the discussions and planning as valued," she concluded.

Research Process: The Choice of Narrative

I deeply appreciated the reflective and responsible contributions teacher researcher colleagues like MacLean had made to my understandings of what it means to teach as a researcher. Yet, when I decided to write my data as narratives, I had to acknowledge what that meant.

- They were *my* way of seeing and telling, although they were added to and revised by my colleagues.
- I gave the narratives shape—beginnings and endings. In the classroom they were part of a highly complex enterprise of human interaction and thought, complicated, unbound by time and place.
- I included the conversations with the teacher researchers within the narratives. Their knowledge was important in understanding their teaching.

I chose the particular narratives presented in this chapter because they were representative. I had seen similar behaviors in other teacher researcher's classrooms, and I recognized something in them from my own teaching as a researcher. The elementary school teacher in the next narrative is representative of teacher researchers following the lead of their students to uncover a variety of ways to learn.

NARRATIVE: WEB VARIETY

Students in this second-third-grade multi-age class are rotating through a series of learning centers including three language arts activities and one on geography. The writing group students open their folders and begin. The teacher moves to a student who is filling in a webbing worksheet, a graphic organizer.

"I thought you'd already started writing."

He looks up. "I forgot to prewrite." He shows her a draft with a few lines written on it, which have been extensively crossed out. He is not happy with it and says, "Prewriting tells me what to think."

The teacher smiles and points to the webbing. "Whose thinking is this then?"

"It's *easier* to think." He smiles back. In the center of his web he has written the title "Terror City." He begins to extend his web. The teacher notes his comments.

Another student pulls out an older web from his writing folder. He has drawn a planet in each cluster. Inside each of the planets he has written: "Who, what, when, where." The teacher asks him about the web design. The student says that he intends to write about each planet separately, giving information about each. His web was helping him organize.

Later, the teacher talks with me about the evolution of her research. She began the year wanting to improve her teaching of writing. At first she gave the students prewriting strategies. This helped some students, but not all. Some began writing without any visible prewriting.

She then became interested in the various adaptations they made to a webbing worksheet she had prepared for them and began collecting the variations that the students created. Her research enabled her to reserve judgment about her students' writing strategies, to collect rather than limit them. She shares the various strategies with the class, so that all the students benefit.

Narrative Discussion: Web Variety

The teacher researcher has used her research in her teaching and vice versa. She began with an interest in writing. The process through which her question evolved led her and her students to explore many different ways to start writing.

Because of her need as a researcher to observe how (and if) her students were prewriting, her classroom management moved from control-focused to observation-focused. She originally had planned a series of prewriting strategies that all students would use. As she observed, however, she saw that different students benefited from different strategies and even invented some of their own.

Research Process: Findings as Narrative

Without knowledge of the context of this teacher researcher's evolving research question about writing, understanding of her research would be lost. Similarly, my listing characteristics of researchers' teaching, however much revised, involved stripping away context specifics and simplifying the connections between the components of the list. Instead, I have ended up with another narrative, more general, the story of a year of teaching as a teacher researcher. The specific classroom narratives that have preceded this more general one are the sources and the illustrations. The quotations are from teacher researchers in the story.

In the fall, the teacher researchers asked their students questions about how and why they learn, questions that they chose because of their interest in them. By questioning, the teacher researchers demonstrated to their students the habits of a researcher. The teacher researchers began to view researching as a way of learning, a process that helped them figure things out.

To investigate their research questions, the teacher researchers observed, listened, and responded to what happened in their classrooms as data. They observed their students, but also observed themselves in action. They became "more alert to their teaching experiences." They recorded, collected, and examined student and teacher words, actions, and artifacts.

Through observing and listening, they achieved a professional distance that paradoxically brought them closer to their students. The students "sense that you are for them. You're working on this issue, something that's not clicking. It's not personal, against them. It gives them a distance too." Both teachers and students recognized that they contributed to the classroom curriculum by discussing the way they learn and that mistakes and errors offered valuable information. Students who were "stuck" offered the class the opportunity to reanalyze what was being learned and how to do it.

In the winter, reviewing their data as it accumulated, the teacher researchers saw differences and similarities among learners and learning situations. They compared their ways of learning with those of their students. Teachers and students both viewed learning as dependent on many variables operating at the same time. Together they developed a repertoire of learning strategies for a variety of learning situations. Planning for this variety meant that teachers stayed alert to connections between what needed to be learned and the students' knowledge and background. Both teachers and students developed confidence that there were ways to learn if they kept trying.

In the early spring, when the research process moved toward analysis and writing, the teacher researchers figured out what they had learned. They and their students articulated theories about teaching and learning and related their actions to their ideas. The teachers planned to teach differently as a result of their research analysis.

In the late spring, when the school year was drawing to a close, teacher researchers saw new questions to ask. As they finished writing up their research reports, they saw that research, like learning, has a product— information, findings, results, interpretations—but it is also a continuing process. They saw research as a developing, changing body of knowledge constantly undergoing revision. They began to view teaching as a process of conducting research even when they were not conducting a formal study related to a specific question.

One year's narrative provides the essentials, but teacher researchers' lives are full of questions and changes, as this middle school math teacher illustrates.

NARRATIVE: MORE QUESTIONS

The classroom is full of student-made posters. There are prints modeled after those of the artist, M. C. Escher and posters showing "Math of Africa," "Math of Japan," and "Math of Arabia." A sign reads "Believe in Yourself." As I come in, the teacher tells me excitedly, in an aside, that one of her female students "just walked in and beat everybody" at a recent math competition.

The students are doing a "math challenge" as a warm-up, a short assignment used at the beginning of a class to get everyone settled and focused. Seated in small groups at tables, they also take turns reporting to the teacher on their homework.

There is a secondary buzz of conversation in the room about the changed schedule. The teacher notices and says, "Look at your schedule. We've changed things around a bit." The school is experimenting with block scheduling. As the students begin their timed practices preparing for a timed test, they realize that the clocks are stopped. They finish anyway, check their answers, and store their practice sheets in their math folders.

"It's new for me to have them talking," she says to me after class, referring to the cooperative learning group strategy she is using, one she learned from another teacher researcher in her group. We begin packing up and raise our voices to be heard over the noise of the school renovation. We are required to leave the building a few minutes after the students.

She mentions her interest in another teacher's research about how block scheduling affects learning disabled students. Then she returns to her current research on girls' math achievement. She made it her topic for the "Following an Issue" research her students are doing as part of a yearlong research project resulting ultimately in a museum display.

Finally, she mentions her questions about how math learning survives, or doesn't, over time. She describes a class that seemed to have very little knowledge of fractions. She knew these students had been taught fractions; she did not blame their former teachers. Instead, she said, "What happens? I'd like to know." She sighs and adds, "You also need to see personal things that are going on."

Narrative Discussion: More Questions

This teacher conducted her research along with her students and was able to discuss research strategies with them. The effect on her of other teacher researchers in her group was evident in her changes to her teaching with their support.

With her research group as a resource she also developed new questions and found even more within school issues and programs. Through teacher research she can individualize and study changes rather than simply accept or resent them.

Research Process: Final Connections

The support of trusted colleagues in a research group gave teacher researchers a chance to analyze what they did as teachers, and to understand their relationship with their students. Even when a lesson went wrong, when a student was angry and recalcitrant, when a community or world disaster overtook the school, or when a teacher had to struggle for energy and strength, the research process offered both the students and their teachers a way toward understanding.

In my earlier research with the students (see Chapter 4) I had learned what principles they saw as essential to teaching for learning. In the present study I learned how teacher researchers shape their teaching as they research. There were similarities in the student ideas about teaching and the teaching of the teacher researchers. Both respected the individuality of the learner. Both knew that learning was a process that included mistakes and errors and saw error as a way of understanding learning. Both invented new learning strategies and shared them to help others learn. Teaching as a researcher gave teachers and their students some commonalities, regardless of their differences.

Being in a teacher researcher classroom gave everyone—students, teachers, and observers—a chance to see what learning looks like, to learn how it is done, to do it. Sanford once remarked that it is not that researching makes you a good teacher, but that it gives you ways to learn how to be one. Although everything did not always go well in their classrooms, the teacher researchers approached their students with a respect and an interest in learning that their students could reciprocate, and this, in turn, made it possible for them to learn together.

REFERENCES

Clandinin, D. J., & Connelly, F. M. (2000). *Narrative inquiry: Experience and story in qualitative research*. San Francisco: Jossey-Bass.

Fecho, B. (2003). Yeki bood/yeki na bood: Writing and publishing as a teacher researcher. *Research in the Teaching of English, 37*(2), 281–293.

Stock, P. L. (1995). *The dialogic curriculum: Teaching and learning in a multicultural society*. Westport, CT: Heinemann-Boynton/Cook.

CHAPTER 7

Coming Into Focus:
How Teacher Researchers Learn

Courtney Rogers

It's like focusing a microscope: you go in and out until you finally zero in on it and it begins to take form.

—Sally Bryan

"Why are you continuing as teacher researchers this year?" Betsy Sanford asked the seven teachers gathered in the Lemon Road Elementary School library on an August afternoon the week before students returned. Vicki Ellison, teacher of second and third graders, explained the effect of her research the year before. "[It] opened my eyes to ways kids learn and think." She noted that it also helped her see changes she wanted to make in her teaching and that she valued the interaction with her teacher researcher colleagues. Chris Saborio spoke of his research with fourth through sixth graders as "challenging"—a way to "focus in on one particular issue I had questions [about] and . . . draw on all the resources and support of other teachers."

I had heard similar comments about the learning that resulted from their research and their work with colleague teacher researchers in meetings with these teachers the preceding year and with teacher researchers in other school groups over a number of years. I wanted to get a clearer picture of how conducting classroom research and participating in a school research group helped "open their eyes," to understand how they learned as individual researchers and as a research group.

Before the conversation moved on to a proposed calendar of group meetings, I explained that I wanted to document what happened during the year as they conducted research and worked together. I planned to collect data as I helped Sanford provide support for the group. The teachers assured me that they would support me in my research, and they did so generously and with great thoughtfulness.

The title of this chapter comes from an observation Sally Bryan made to her colleagues the following spring as they shared results of their research and insights about the process that had led to their findings. Using the microscope metaphor, Bryan described her experience with data analysis as it moved her gradually toward understanding.

DATA COLLECTION AND ANALYSIS

Lemon Road Elementary School was the smallest elementary school in the district with 11 full-time classroom teachers and a diverse population of fewer than 300 students. Even though the research group included a majority of the staff the first year, teacher researchers were creating a new community within the school. In the group's second year 7 of the 10 teachers from the first year chose to participate again, and 1 new teacher joined.

They met about every 3 weeks to talk about their research, share and puzzle over their classroom data, and help each other make decisions about next steps. I met regularly with Sanford to help plan meetings, discuss issues, and later in the year read and respond to research drafts. I attended the group meetings, helped with activities, and conferred with teachers about their work. I recorded observations and reflections on meetings, events, and conversations and conducted individual interviews with Sanford and three of the teacher researchers. In addition, I had access to a variety of documents and correspondence generated by the work of the group.

To my analysis of the data, I brought not only the perspective of one involved in a support role but also experience as a teacher researcher and facilitator of other school-based groups. I regarded my lens of experience with both respect and wariness. My knowledge of teacher research and research groups in schools helped me to recognize significant details and subtleties that would not have been evident to me years before. However, my perspective also included assumptions and beliefs that would influence how I understood what I saw.

I used two strategies to address potential bias in my interpretation of data. First, I discussed the data and my analysis of it with the Planning Group, using their knowledge to help focus my interpretations. Second, I shared data and analysis with the Lemon Road teacher researchers, asking them to confirm, challenge, revise, correct, or elaborate on my perceptions. Two sets of data—the individual interviews and the discussions at research group meetings—were central to what I learned.

RESEARCH AS LEARNING: INDIVIDUAL STORIES

While my intent was to learn all that I could from the entire research group, I collected more data from some participants than others. About halfway through the year, I interviewed Ellison and Saborio after first observing in their classrooms. I also interviewed school counselor Sandy Wolin-Bromley. I asked them questions about their

- Experiences as researchers and effects on their practice
- Research in the context of professional development
- Work with fellow teacher researchers
- Experiences in the second year as compared to the first

Vicki Ellison

When she talked about her research, Ellison consistently used sight as a metaphor for learning—a metaphor that appeared also in the observations of her research colleagues:

> [Conducting research] makes me focus on what exactly it is I'm trying to do with kids and what's really most important. . . . It's taking the time to take a look at what's going on . . . and then trying to take what you see and make changes for the better.

In her first year Ellison studied what happened when students in her multiage second- and third-grade classroom chose their own spelling words. Concerned about the new spelling program adopted at her school and discouraged about disappointing results on the students' first spelling test, Ellison decided to "take a close look at the new program in our classroom, try to work out the kinks, and at the same time learn about my students' choices" in spelling. In addition to collecting data as students worked on spelling, Ellison interviewed them throughout the year to understand why and how they chose their words and the strategies they used to learn them.

Analysis of the data, she explained in her research report, "opened my eyes to different aspects of students and their learning." She saw that students chose words that had meaning or relevance to them; that they took pride in learning "hard" words; that they valued the autonomy she allowed; and that they could "develop strategies they need in order to spell a word." She also found that students' performance on spelling assessments improved. The biggest impact of her research on her teaching was that she began to talk more with her students about their learning. She asked more questions of her students, such as "What do you think?" or "Why did you do that?"

The second year Ellison turned her attention to the role of student talk as they worked in groups. She experienced "difficulty coming up with ways to collect data" and worried that her current research fell short of the standard she had set in her first-year study. Using tape recorders to capture their conversation during group work, however, she again discovered that her young students could "take a critical look at their work" as she would later write in her report:

> Conversations among my students revealed that they self-monitor their work for mistakes and organization; check their progress; and compare current work to that previously completed.

Ellison believed that her research informed her assessment of individual student progress, her decisions about instruction, her thinking about educational philosophy, and her sense of her own role in the learning of her students. "In addition to looking and listening more carefully to my students, I'm also doing the same thing to myself":

> Conducting research makes you take the time to think about what you're doing and to kind of chart the course according to what happens and what you notice and the reactions or responses that your kids have. So it's like having an out of body experience because I'm looking at myself in the classroom from outside myself.

Ellison the researcher was studying Ellison the teacher as well as her students and their interactions.

She distinguished teacher research from other forms of staff development in that she determined the focus of her own learning. She valued the opportunity to tailor her research topic to her professional needs and to learn from colleagues who also selected their own research topics.

> I really enjoyed talking to other teachers about what's going on in their classrooms and what's going on with mine and getting feedback and giving feedback. . . . They're usually working on topics that are different from mine, so it gives me the opportunity to learn more about whatever subjects they choose.

She noted the value of the support from her research colleagues who were "willing to listen and give feedback when needed." She added, "I think this year we're more used to those roles and perhaps it comes a little more naturally."

By the second year what Ellison had learned in her spelling research informed not only her own teaching but also the practices of some of her colleagues who adapted some of her strategies to their classrooms. In addition to presenting her research at the regional Teacher Researcher Conference, Ellison published her study on spelling in a nationally circulated professional journal, making her learning accessible to a broader public.

Chris Saborio

In his second year of research, Saborio described himself as "more relaxed" because he was less concerned about "doing it right" and ready to "take more risks." "It took the second year for me to overcome . . . being concerned about whether my [research] question was good enough. . . . Once I let go of that," he explained, "[I became] more open to help from my peers" and "learned a lot more about myself as a teacher."

Saborio documented what happened when he gave his students with learning disabilities greater responsibility for decisions about how they learned social studies content and how their learning was evaluated. It was part of a movement toward "empowering" students, something he said he has "always believed in, but you start with a belief and then you . . . have to learn how to put that in practice." For this direction in his teaching he gave a large measure of credit to interaction with his teacher researcher colleagues.

"I'm drawn to being collaborative," Saborio explained; "that's probably why I signed up for teacher research."

> I respond really well to . . . focusing on an issue as an individual but also doing it as part of a team. We all have our own individual questions, but we're a team of teacher researchers getting support, getting help as we work our way through questions that we've picked. . . . It also makes my work seem more valuable because it becomes more public.

Saborio said that the kind of collaboration that occurs in the research group should be "built in" as a regular part of teachers' professional exchange in a school.

"What I'm learning about myself as a teacher I'm learning by doing and then reflecting with colleagues during teacher research meetings." The questions and reflections of other researchers about his research helped him make sense of his teaching. "It's like reflection in action—you're a teacher researcher, you're reflecting as you go along and . . . the [other] person keeps bouncing it back to you," Saborio explained.

Saborio's reflection includes both mirroring back to one's colleague and critical reseeing of past events in the classroom. For example, he described his efforts to give students more decision making as "something I may not have come to try as quickly if I were just doing everything on my own."

Because of the opportunities to analyze classroom events with his colleagues, he said, "I'm learning about myself," how to try something and "then look at what I'm doing to contribute to a situation." Teacher research gave him the distance to be self-critical and analytical.

When Saborio talked about his frustration with student behavior during a spelling lesson I had observed in his classroom, he remarked, "Maybe I should have Betsy [Sanford] come in and videotape them." A research strategy had become a teaching strategy—a way to collect data on student behavior that later, from a distance, could be analyzed with a colleague for its teaching implications.

He explained how the process works in the research group meetings:

> You don't feel . . . in these meetings that you have to fix [someone else's issue] although I did feel that way at the beginning. . . . I was thinking . . . last year when I was in the middle of trying to fix people's problems, that that's the wrong way to do it . . . because what winds up happening is they really don't . . . learn that much about themselves.

Saborio's view that one cannot answer someone else's questions, cannot learn for someone else, carried over into directions he was taking in his teaching and his work with his students. "Before teacher research, I think I put a lot of energy into forcing kids to do things a certain way or my way," he observed.

Saborio also recognized the power of self-selection of research topic. A research question he is "truly interested in" results in his "going . . . the extra yard to figure it out because it's . . . very pertinent to my life." He controls the direction of his own learning, but he recognizes the influence of his colleagues on his thinking and his practice.

Also like Ellison, he noted differences between the learning that occurs in a course and in the research group:

> I loved grad school, I love taking courses . . . but it's different outside of your classroom. What's nice about teacher research is [that] you go outside of your classroom, but you're bringing your classroom into that environment as opposed to learning *about* your classroom as a separate entity.

The "environment" he describes is the circle of colleagues in his research group who help him look back into his classroom to understand it.

When asked about the effects of the research group on other teachers in the school, Saborio told a story about how his research had a direct impact on a colleague who was not in the research group. In a team-teaching situation he suggested to his colleague the use of a strategy he had explored through his research, crediting his willingness to suggest the alternative to his research experience. Like Ellison, he presented his research at the Teacher Researcher Conference.

Sandy Wolin-Bromley

Counselor Wolin-Bromley said that she felt "insecure" about her research the first year:

> I didn't know—what do you want from me? What am I supposed
> to do? . . . It was not comfortable. . . . There was a tentative
> nature to the group which was okay because we were all in the
> same experience, but it didn't help to ease my anxiety until I myself
> lived through the process. . . . Once I decided that it was okay to
> be me within this process, it was much easier.

In her research article she reported the findings from her study at the same time that she candidly described her discomfort with a research process that felt uncertain and unpredictable. She began with a broad question about what caused lack of motivation in students—a question she was reluctant to let go despite the "counsel" of her colleagues that it appeared "too complicated and far-reaching in its scope." She believed that she "could not change course." Eventually she realized, as she wryly admitted, "I could not investigate this question . . . and hope to complete the research within my lifetime."

As she continued to interview students and observe them in classrooms, Wolin-Bromley turned her question around and made it manageable. "What do teachers do to help you learn?" she asked the students. During the course of her study she "had become a researcher no longer threatened by changing the course of my research."

Wolin-Bromley seemed more comfortable with the discomfort of the process in her second year. She wrote in her report:

> Only after many drafts of possible questions and a great deal of
> help from my colleagues did I experience that comfortable feeling
> that comes to the teacher researcher when she knows she has
> found her question.

Her question focused on what she learned when she studied her own work with a weekly support group for fifth- and sixth-grade students who were consistently not completing their homework assignments. Writing her research paper the second year seemed more difficult because she was a more skilled researcher who had generated "a lot more data." She found that the students learned to listen carefully and respectfully to one another, gave support to their peers, challenged unproductive behaviors in a non-threatening manner, and exerted pressure on each other to make positive changes. Over time most of the students completed their assignments and took responsibility for their choices when they did not.

Wolin-Bromley talked about a kind of distance that it was important for her to establish between her goals with the students and her research. "I believed that the only way my research would be successful was that all of these kids were better at the end of the year." She described as a relief the realization that her research did not, indeed, confer that obligation. To herself she gave the following advice: "Wherever the kids are, that's where they are. And I have to listen, . . . I have to see where I can maybe help them rethink or revisit something . . . [without] the goal of fixing it because then what that says is *I'm* so wonderful . . . *I* can make it better." Like Saborio, Wolin-Bromley used the research lens to view her own role from a different perspective.

Like Ellison and Saborio, Wolin-Bromley valued both the private and the public nature of learning in the research process. She explained how the experience suited her preferences. "I cannot sit in classes. . . . This is a process where I can dialogue with people, and I have autonomy." She said about the support she receives from group leader Sanford: "I know that I can always call on her to discuss anything. I believe she has to be in the role of, not expert, but someone who knows more than I [about conducting research]."

She also characterized the dialogue with colleagues at research meetings:

> Our process is conversational. . . . There's a commitment to kids in this group . . . a consistent commitment. . . . I make an assumption that the people who do this really care about what they're doing, and I respect that a great deal; . . . the dialogue in this group is . . . serious.

Wolin-Bromley insisted on her own professional interest and her commitment to her students as the primary motivations for her research. At the same time, she expressed interest in publishing her work to a wider audience and shared her findings in a public forum at the local Teacher Researcher Conference.

RESEARCH AS LEARNING: GROUP MEETINGS

While the progress of each teacher's research followed its own timeline, Sanford designed meetings for the group to support one another through a research process: uncovering questions, collecting and analyzing data, drafting and writing to discover findings and identify implications. In addition to regular 2-hour sessions every 3 weeks after school, the group gathered for three all-day meetings in October, November, and April, two of them held jointly with the other two schools in the project. Each researcher had a full day of leave for writing a research draft in March.

The dialogue with colleagues that teacher researchers said was critical to their learning occurred as spontaneous informal conversations next to the school copier, individual check-in meetings or conferences with leader Sanford, and discussions at regular meetings of the group. Reflective writing in research logs and sharing of classroom data were companions to the talk about their research methods and projects as they unfolded. From the dialogue at meetings emerge some of the same themes that appear in the interviews with Ellison, Saborio, and Wolin-Bromley.

Collegial Conversation: Developing Community and Confidence

An all-day session early in October revealed evidence of the developing learning community that teachers had described in interviews. The day included reading of first-year research reports, discussion of connections across studies and findings, plans for sharing those findings with the school staff, and exploration of second-year research questions and data.

"This is the first time in my life that I really didn't mind reading research articles," quipped Wolin-Bromley. Respect for the learning of their colleagues was evident as teachers cited and cross-referenced observations and findings from their research studies. As they talked, they began to identify themes across studies and implications for their teaching. Sanford articulated one of these themes—the value of listening to students—as she summarized what she had heard in teachers' comments:

> Students have important things to contribute. They can share their learning strategies. It isn't just that if you're a good teacher you should respect what your students say; it's that you can't teach without it.

While the teachers seemed confident of their observations to one another, they seemed less sure that what they had learned would be considered of value by their colleagues beyond the research group. They talked for some time about how they might share their research with other teachers in the school. "How will it best be received? In what format will it be heard?" asked Wolin-Bromley. Eventually they decided to invite staff to meet with them on a Monday after school to talk about their findings and to receive a copy of their collected written reports.

Saborio suggested they use the roundtable discussion format from the Teacher Researcher Conference:

> We could make a miniconference, invite staff to participate and then at each roundtable get the discussion going. I think if we put requirements on people, we're not treating them as colleagues.

His comment seemed to reflect a recognition that the community they were creating was characterized by mutual respect that needed to extend to the school community.

Later teachers turned attention to their current research as they announced how they wanted to spend the next portion of the meeting:

> *Ellison*: I need 15 minutes or so in a corner to listen to some data I've recorded.
> *Saborio*: I need some time to look at data—what happens when LD kids are integrated with regular ed[ucation] cooperative learning groups.

Others explained to their colleagues and themselves where they thought they were with their research:

> I think I know what my question is—how to motivate kids in writing. I need to collect data. . . .

> I just get more mixed up instead of less. I started wanting to look at computers and the classroom . . . but I want to look at . . . "What knowledge do I have as an ESOL teacher that would help teachers in the classroom?"

Another researcher stated, "I need talking time. I don't really have a question; what I really have is frustration," she explained, about students who appeared to return from summer vacation having lost the learning from the previous year. Leader Sanford said that she needed some time with her own data on first-grade math learning but that she would first respond to her colleague's request for talk.

Careful listening—both to one another and to oneself—seemed important. Although teachers were in different places in their research process, the talk supported them as they figured out the next steps.

Supportive Dialogue: Making Sense of Data

The theme for a February research meeting was data analysis. When they arrived, the teachers found newsprint, crayons, and magic markers at their tables. Guest researcher Marian Mohr asked them to try a strategy for making sense of their data as a whole: "Take about ten minutes to make a picture of your research, putting all your data on one page. Just see what happens."

Some researchers immediately put crayon to paper while others approached their blank sheets tentatively. After a few minutes, each shared results with the group. Wolin-Bromley admitted that she had resisted the task but that it forced her to confront what seemed an overwhelming amount of data. Showing her picture to the group, she explained:

> These are the major themes [of the student homework support group]. First . . . support and unity and connectedness and camaraderie. So we're all in this circle. . . . The next thing is talking, sharing, really listening, and observing—these kids are incredible at making observations. Openness and honesty. Then I thought of confrontation or challenging behaviors, and the kids are great at that in a really decent way. Then encouragement, praise, acknowledgment. When the kids receive it, it's incredible, and it's a big piece of what goes on, I think, to help them do better. . . . These are just the themes of what I'm seeing, and I don't know how I'm going to write it out as . . . findings.

A discussion of her drawing and her description of it followed.

Mohr (pointing to her picture): Is that a light bulb?
Wolin-Bromley (nodding): Awareness, which I think is the first step for change, and I was thinking that even if just some of the kids who don't change their behaviors this year know there's a problem, maybe they'll change eventually.
Colleague: Can I ask a question? Do the behaviors that you see in . . . your group—do you observe those same behaviors in their respective classrooms? I mean I'm wondering if—"
Wolin-Bromley: No, it's a totally different environment . . . and I think it's safe . . .
Colleague: They trust you . . .
Wolin-Bromley: And I think they trust each other in the group.

Sanford restated what she understood to be Wolin-Bromley's research question, pointing out that she was already deriving findings from her data.

A relieved Wolin-Bromley explained how anxious she had been about making sense of her data and thanked Sanford. Her colleagues continued to ask questions and offer observations that helped her consider her research data, approaches to analysis, and ways to present findings and implications.

Conversation after everyone had shared their visualizations returned to a theme from the October discussion of common findings—the importance of teachers listening to what students have to say about their learning. One teacher explained: "You find out what they need, and you find out what they know when you ask questions." Teachers nodded in agreement when Ellison talked about what happened in her research:

> It's . . . their chance to help us learn. They're . . . teaching us. Because when I have my whole group interviews, they all raise their hands. They all want to say something, and maybe part of that is because it's their chance to tell me something, to open my eyes to something.

Teachers valued the learning that came from their dialogue with their colleagues and their students.

Honest Talk: Listening and Looking Carefully

To an all-day meeting in April I brought copies of a list of observed behaviors of the teachers as researchers in their second year. I asked each person to indicate on the list which of the behaviors seemed accurate descriptions. A discussion followed as the teachers responded and offered their own observations about their experiences.

Saborio commented about the group talk, "I think it's easier for us to communicate now and share our ideas because we all have a . . . common understanding of what we're trying to do." Others indicated agreement. Sanford elaborated:

> I have noticed over and over this year that the type of talk seems different in quality from last year. People are much quicker to get right into it about teaching and learning. . . . We have a history with each other now . . . but it's also that we have put on the table what some of this . . . really means to each of us.

The honest, probing talk—being able "to put on the table" questions and issues that matter—contributed to growing trust and respect for each other and for research as a way of learning.

Commenting that she felt teachers' anxiety about the research process got in the way of "talking honestly" during the first year, Wolin-Bromley

suggested that in the second year "maybe we're looking honestly at ourselves [asking] 'Are we really doing what we say we're doing?'" Wolin-
Bromley described conducting research as resulting in "more of an awareness" for teachers that they are using a particular strategy "for a purpose."
Previously, as teachers, "we didn't really question—we just did it, and now
we're doing it and we're listening with that extra ear."

She elaborated on the effects of looking and listening as a researcher
when working with students:

> Being a teacher researcher makes one more aware of the nuances
> of behavior in relationship to learning. . . . I know I've become
> more accepting because of this process of researching. . . . I don't
> look at a behavior [as] necessarily negative. It's information."

She cited a student who, during instruction, "looks all over the place, but
he's listening to everything. So it's okay if he does that. . . ."

Colleague Sally Bryan agreed that as a teacher researcher she is "looking more carefully and seeing the children more as a whole":

> If they're unable to do something, instead of saying, "Well, you got
> that wrong," you say, "Now wait a minute, what is going on here
> that this child didn't get it? Did I not teach this well? Obviously I
> have to revisit it."

Bryan also compared writing about her research for her first and second
studies. The first year she felt she "had to solve the educational problems
of the world" with her report. With her second study, she described herself
as more comfortable with "no answer this year, but . . . getting closer to an
answer."

Seasoned researcher Sanford observed that, regardless of the researcher's past experiences, every research venture carries with it a large measure
of uncertainty:

> I do have some trust in the research process but [also] . . . I'm will-
> ing to take a risk. I wasn't sure that I would figure out anything
> about math this year, but I was willing to risk it. . . . [I felt] there's
> a chance I'm going to learn.

Sanford's comment reminded me that it takes courage to do the work these
teachers were doing. It requires their willingness to live with ambiguity and
uncertainty and with the possibility of failing to gain the desired insight or
understanding.

FINDINGS

I began my research knowing that teacher researchers value their research experiences and their interactions with research colleagues. Looking closely at the Lemon Road teacher researchers in their second year, I saw them develop respect for the research process as a way of learning about their teaching and for themselves and their colleagues as learners and knowers.

Developing Trust in Research Learning

Teachers developed respect for research as a way of learning as they gained skills and experience with the process. Wolin-Bromley, Saborio, and Bryan suggested that part of what contributes to greater tolerance for the uncertainty was developing a measure of confidence in one's own ability to negotiate the process. For Wolin-Bromley, it meant knowing what to expect and defining it in terms she could understand and manage. For Saborio, it required the courage to make public ideas and concerns that might not be seen as "great" or "right" to others. For Bryan, it was accepting the notion that learning does not mean getting all the answers once and for all.

These teacher researchers asked questions that mattered to them and remained open to what they discovered, even when it was uncomfortable or disappointing. Their skills as researchers and their commitment to learning enabled them to hear and see their students and themselves in ways that led to new understandings of what it means to teach and learn.

Research Learning: Public and Private, Collaborative and Self-Directed

Teachers valued the opportunity to shape their professional growth to fit their learning needs and those of their particular students. They formed their questions out of what was happening in their own practice and invited their colleagues to help them make sense of what they saw. The learning was not "outside" their classroom experience but grew directly from it. Temporarily stepping away from their bustling classrooms, they brought pieces of what happened there to examine with their colleagues in a trusted public space. Gradually, they began to recognize the importance of their findings and implications for classrooms beyond their own, and shared their work with others at Lemon Road and at professional conferences.

Understanding Through Managed Distance

As teachers became more comfortable with looking closely at and listening carefully to their students and themselves, they did so less judgmentally and more analytically. As they collected and evaluated data from their classrooms over time, they avoided premature interpretation or hasty conclusions that might cloud the whole truth of what was happening. They learned, as Wolin-Bromley explained, to see a student behavior as "information" to be added to other data in their search for understanding.

Ellison described as an "out-of-body experience" the practice of looking "more carefully" at herself in the classroom from outside herself. Saborio explained how his colleagues helped him "reflect" back on events from his classroom to make sense of them. Wolin-Bromley talked about the kind of distance she needed between what she wanted to happen for her students and what actually occurred, the space that allows "looking honestly at ourselves." The research stance—a kind of managed distance from their classrooms and their practice—promoted constructive self-reflection and self-criticism.

Creating a Learning Community

As teacher researchers supported each other in their research, they created a community that offered support for honest, meaningful dialogue about teaching and learning. In the company of their colleagues, teacher researchers asked questions about teaching and learning for which they did not have answers. The conversation in their meetings demonstrated their respect for one another and for the research knowledge they created individually and collectively.

At their last meeting of the year in June, Bryan said that when you conduct research "you end up being a better teacher." She and her colleagues stated unequivocally that the knowledge they generate in their research is valuable to them and to their students, that the struggle to make sense of their classrooms is worth the risks and the effort. It is in the context of a group, with the support and recognition of their colleagues, that teachers gain confidence in their own learning and its value to others. Once we "feel on solid ground in terms of the real significance of our work," Sanford speculated, "we would feel confident enough about the significance of what we're doing that we would start working for school change."

QUESTIONS AND IMPLICATIONS

Teacher researchers, from Lemon Road and other schools, have commented that what distinguishes the dialogue in their groups from other conversations in schools is its honesty—about what happens in classrooms and about what teachers know and do not know. These comments suggest that the culture of schools has discouraged the concept of teachers as learners. Ellison and I talked, for example, about the fact that new teachers perceive that they are expected to arrive at their schools "in the know." Messages they receive, usually unspoken, may lead them to conclude, "What I don't know I will pretend to know or keep quiet about or try to figure out on my own. And if I do figure it out, I must remember that I'm not supposed to know any more than my colleagues." In many schools it is difficult to be honest with one's colleagues about either position: knowing or not knowing.

How is it that our schools have become places where teachers do not feel respected as knowers or supported as learners? And how can we expect these same adults to create environments that help students grow as learners and knowers? Teacher researchers model for their students and colleagues a concept of learning that includes openly asking and systematically investigating questions that matter to them about teaching and learning. They will need to educate others in their profession not only about the value of their research findings but also about the value of the research process as it leads to improved teaching and learning.

How Does Teacher Research Affect Schools?

Part III presents our studies of how teacher research affects schools beyond the classroom context. Chapter 8, "Roles and Relationships: Principals and Teacher Researcher Leaders," examines the developing and changing relationship between principals and teacher research group leaders. Chapter 9, "Not Entirely by Design: Teacher Research and School Planning," is a study of the overlapping and intermingling of a teacher research group with the ongoing work of school planning and evaluation.

Chapter 10, "The Leaven in the Loaf: Teacher Research Knowledge in Schools," pulls together data from many different teacher researchers and different schools to describe how teacher research knowledge works its way from the classroom outward into the school as a whole. Chapter 11, "Teacher Researcher Leadership," focuses on the three teacher research group leaders and how they and their colleagues perceive their way of leading the groups. Chapter 12, "A Teacher Researcher Network," traces the development of the network of teacher researchers, showing how the teacher researchers, as professionals, affect the school district.

CHAPTER 8

Roles and Relationships: Principals and Teacher Researcher Leaders

Mary Ann Nocerino

I saw right away that it grew out of teachers' desire to improve student learning.

—Marvin Spratley

We knew that principals had to approve and actively support the teacher researcher projects in their schools. But how they came to do this, and how the relationships between the principals and the teacher researcher leaders unfolded, gave new meaning to our understanding about leadership and the roles of teachers and principals in school change.

BACKGROUND

We believed that the school is the basic unit of change in education and that teachers play a fundamental role in schools. We also believed that knowledge gained from teachers' research not only informs their own teaching, but can shape their school as well as their district-level programs and policies.

We knew about the importance of the principal's role in facilitating school change from our reading and from our experiences as teachers, resource specialists, and central office administrators. Perhaps Courtney Rogers and I had learned most profoundly from our work with more than 130 school teams of teachers, parents, and administrators in collaborative school-based planning and evaluation projects. From our experiences with these groups, we had noticed several factors we believed supported the successful implementation of a meaningful and useful school planning process. I mention two of these factors to identify the lens through which I viewed the principals and teacher researcher leaders in relation to the teacher researcher communities in their schools.

One factor is related to school culture and the second is related to school organization. Schools are more likely to have a meaningful planning and decision-making process when the culture recognizes teacher knowledge and capacity for figuring out ways to improve student achievement and to evaluate progress. The second factor is linked to the first—successful schools establish an organizational structure for planning and sharing knowledge among teachers and administrators, one which ensures opportunity and purpose both for disseminating information and making decisions.

THE THREE SCHOOLS

Each of the three project schools had an experienced teacher researcher on staff who was willing to make a 3-year commitment to the project. Each school also had a principal who was supportive of teacher leadership. Even though initially the principals had little or no knowledge of teacher research, they recognized the potential of the project and were willing to support it in their schools. All three of the schools were highly diverse linguistically, economically, racially, culturally, and academically. In addition to white, African, and Asian Americans, many students were recent arrivals from countries all over the world. Nearly half of the students in the three schools were from families where the primary language spoken at home was one other than English.

The entire staff at each of the three schools was informed about the project, and all teachers were invited to join the teacher research group. Six to ten teachers responded in each of the schools, and thus the project began—with small groups quietly discovering what teacher research was all about.

DATA COLLECTION

I collected data from a variety of sources that included notes from individual interviews with principals, notes and minutes from Planning Group meetings, field notes from project activities, and taped and transcribed group interviews with the principals. Since the principals we needed to talk with had very full schedules, we decided to combine data collection with lunch. Lunch was prepared by the Planning Group members and included gourmet chicken salad, sesame noodles, fresh asparagus vinaigrette, and other un-cafeteria-like fare in a quiet room away from their schools. We all enjoyed the experience.

I reviewed the data periodically as the project unfolded to determine categories, patterns, and themes. Ongoing review and analysis of the data were also conducted during our Planning Group meetings which we audiotaped. The Planning Group and the principals reviewed various stages of my draft for accuracy of content.

THE EMERGENCE OF TWO MAJOR THEMES

As I studied the data, two major themes emerged: (a) principals understood the impact of teacher research differently; and (b) principals and teacher researcher leaders developed a reciprocal relationship.

Understanding the Impact of Teacher Research

The principals all observed that teacher research is beneficial for students and recognized that teacher research had a profound impact on the professional development of teachers. However, they differed in the emphasis they placed on the impact of the project in such areas as curriculum development, staff development, student achievement, collegiality, and school planning. The following is a look at how the principals' visions for teacher research developed and at their perceptions of the impact of a teacher researcher project in their schools.

Lemon Road Elementary School. During the project, Lemon Road Elementary School had the distinction of being the smallest school in the district with a student population of under 300 and 11 classroom teachers. Because of the small number of students it had been threatened with closing. Carolyn Williams, a first-time principal, was assigned to Lemon Road 15 months before the project began.

In the initial project interview, Williams, as a new principal to Lemon Road, noted that teachers seemed isolated professionally from one another. In subsequent discussions over the 3 years she spoke of the growth of professional conversations among the teachers as a result of the work of the teacher research group. She also saw benefits for teachers and children as well as for school planning.

A year and a half after the project began, during the principal group interview over lunch, she noted:

> I think teacher research is really important in that it gives us a focus
> . . . the conversations take a higher level . . . [teachers] are looking at
> kids and how kids are learning and they look at what's working and
> what's not. There were many surprises. I think that it really just takes
> the whole school to another level; even the teachers who are not
> involved [in research] are . . . benefiting from those conversations.

She also talked about the development of a collective focus on students at Lemon Road.

> We're moving toward being not just a kid-centered school but a kid-centered school with a team of teachers who are all working together. And I'm thinking that through the research and discussions, we are moving away from speaking of students as "These are my ESOL kids" or "These are my LD kids" to [speaking of students as] "These are all of our kids." And because they [teachers] are working and talking and sharing what they're finding, it's working very positively to make it a more unified school.

After the first-year teacher researchers published their findings, Williams recognized the effect that teacher research could have on curriculum in the school. For example, she noted that Vicki Ellison's work on her students' acquisition of spelling skills had implications for teaching spelling in other classrooms, and she saw other teachers in the school begin to use Ellison's research in their work with students.

By the third year, other developments began to take place at Lemon Road. The school established a school planning team consisting of a representative group of teachers and parents and the principal. The purpose of the team was to develop and implement a multiyear school plan, involving the staff in the process. During the principal luncheon interview that year, Williams projected her vision that teacher research would become part of the plan so that the school culture might become one of inquiry for purposes of improving student achievement.

> Basically, I'm hoping that we would get to the point that teacher research will be our umbrella [of the school plan]. . . . The objective would be that [staff] would be looking at their classrooms in a systematic, organized way, that the outcomes will be shared.

Indeed, by the end of the year, the staff collaboratively completed a draft of the school plan with an overarching objective related to classroom inquiry focused on how and what students were learning. The teacher researcher leader, Betsy Sanford, noted that the school was now a place to talk about teaching and learning. This comment illustrates a major shift in the school culture from a place where professional dialogues were infrequent, as observed by the principal upon her appointment to the school, to one where instructional dialogue was a pronounced part of school life.

Poe Middle School. During the 3-year research project, Poe Middle School, which had 860 students, was undergoing renovation. The school had recently adopted the middle school concept and block scheduling. Teams of teachers in the core subjects provided instruction for their group of students. There was a frenetic schedule of team and department meetings and movement around the construction dust. As with many middle schools in the district, teachers and administrators were seeking new ways of working together in interdisciplinary teams and new ways of teaching in larger blocks of time. There was a major turnover in the administrative staff during the 3 years of the project with new appointments for the principal, guidance director, and two assistant principals.

June Monterio began her principal career at Poe one year after the project began. Although she had no previous experience with teacher research, she was very optimistic about the impact it could have on the school.

> You know this is new for me. . . . I'm excited about it . . . [teachers] shared with me the research from last year . . . and I want it to impact on instruction at Poe and to become more of an integral part of the school and the climate.

When developing the organizational chart for the school after serving as principal for one year, she placed the teacher research group as a work group along with the math and reading work groups. In addition, she added their meetings to the school calendar. Both appearances made the teacher research group more visible to the 45 staff members.

Monterio also asked the teacher researcher leader, Sheila Clawson, to talk briefly about teacher research and research findings at each of the monthly faculty meetings. She wanted to inform the teachers about the findings and also to interest them in the work of the group. She saw teacher research as a staff development model and the teacher researcher leader as a resource person for staff development.

Monterio articulated her vision for teacher research at the school:

> My vision was for the research to impact the school through staff development avenues, and I think we're beginning to do that . . . to provide in-house staff development as a result of some of the research of the research team.

Monterio also asked Clawson to provide training for staff on cooperative learning and assessment. Only some of the content of this training was an outgrowth of her recent research. The principal had identified the teacher researcher leader's skill in instruction and was using her expertise in a more general way, not limiting it to her research skills and knowledge gained from her research. In this way, the principal was advancing her goal of providing school-based staff development. However, throughout the course of the third year of the project, her goal of in-house staff development became overshadowed by school issues related to school teams, interdisciplinary teaching, the teacher advisory program, the gifted and talented program, and block scheduling.

Falls Church High School. Falls Church High School, with 1,300 students, began block scheduling during the third year of the project after the faculty voted to implement it. Marvin Spratley had been the principal for 5 years. The administrators and faculty were in the process of determining how the many departments, standing and ad hoc committees, and differing roles of teachers, administrators, and department chairs might best function. This examination was part of the school accreditation process that emphasized school renewal through collaborative school planning and evaluation.

In the initial project interview with Spratley, he remarked that teachers studying their own practice will improve instruction. He believed that instruction should be the main focus of the high school despite the competing tugs pulling in many directions. Later on in the project Spratley reflected:

> There is so much that competes for teachers' attention from both things inside and outside of the school system. . . . From my perspective, the teacher researcher effort has been a catalyst to keep us focused . . . it's a catalyst for conversation that's associated with instruction. . . . I see it as helping us focus and . . . being a fertile ground for conversations I enjoy. I can talk about gangs, I can talk about transportation, and I can talk about budget, but I don't enjoy that stuff . . . let us talk about instruction.

During the third year of the project (and the end of the first year of block scheduling), the block scheduling committee conducted a survey to assess progress and uncover issues. The survey was developed and analyzed with the leadership provided by the teacher researcher leader of the project, Marion MacLean (see Chapter 9). The honed research skills brought to the task by MacLean facilitated the process of data collection and analysis. Spratley and MacLean attempted to figure out how the skills and knowledge of teacher researchers could be used for school planning and evaluation.

The three principals began with limited or no knowledge about teacher research. However, over the 3 years their understanding of teacher research and their efforts to support the work of the teacher researchers grew. They were willing to learn about and support teacher research. They all communicated effectively, established rapport, demonstrated their willingness to participate fully in give-and-take about ideas, and showed that they gave new ideas serious consideration in their own decision making. They recognized that teacher research had the potential to accomplish their goals for their schools.

Developing Reciprocal Relationships

This section considers the changing relationship and roles of the teacher researcher leaders and the principals as they promoted and sustained teacher research. Rather than addressing the three schools separately, this theme will be discussed across the three schools.

MacLean, teacher researcher leader at Falls Church High School, describes her principal's appreciation of the research group's work as follows:

Our principal read our research book before our very first faculty meeting. . . . He used it as the focus of his speech to the rest of the faculty about keeping the main thing in view, which was instruction. . . . That's what we were doing. . . . It was his way of saying, "This is what matters." And that was a powerful statement (at least to us) that he got it, that he was behind us. He was willing to put himself out in front of other people. . . . He respected our work. . . . He came to our research meeting. He talked to us. . . . He had notes on everybody's research. It was like he knew it—and was just so appreciative of it, and not just in a glossy general way but much more.

In the early stages of the project we were interested in learning about the role of the principal in supporting teacher research. We discovered that the principal and teacher researcher leader were really engaged in exchanges that focused on how the two could support each other in promoting teacher research, each from his or her own position, in a reciprocal and collegial way. These roles are different from the traditional roles that administrators and teachers play where the principal has historically made most decisions for the school while the teachers' role is centered in their classrooms with little influence and power.

Knowledge Exchange and Mutual Trust. The teacher researcher leaders contributed their knowledge of the teacher research process, and the principals contributed their understanding of the overall elements of school organization and dynamics of school operations. Relationships developed between the two of them that allowed issues not directly related to teacher research to be discussed with candor and mutual trust. The relationship became a safe place to talk about issues related to schooling such as staffing, sorting out one's role (principal as well as teacher researcher leader), and community pressures.

The teacher researcher leaders talked about the tensions they sometimes felt in the new relationship—what to say, how to say it, issues of confidentiality, and maintaining their relationship with fellow teachers. Principals mentioned other tensions they felt. Two of the three principals articulated their concerns that teacher researcher leaders might be viewed as "favorites." This perception could be counterproductive to the work of the project, staff, and administrators.

Teacher Researcher Leader Initiative. Principals appreciated the initiative that the teacher researcher leaders took in helping them understand the teacher research process and ways to support the project through regular yet informal conversations. Monterio spoke about the importance of the support of the principal and the teacher researcher leader in sustaining the project and helping to create a school culture for inquiry. She felt that if there were changes in the administrator or teacher researcher staff and there was no one left at the school to provide leadership, the project would die. In actuality, Monterio experienced such a change firsthand because she was the new administrator who inherited the project when she became the school principal during the second year of the project.

> [Clawson] may leave. . . . I may leave, but hopefully [teacher research] will have some impact, and I will be able to pass that on to the next principal. I think that's the only way that it will live, but if there's no enthusiasm from the principal, I think it will die. . . . If someone new should come in . . . someone has to take the initiative. . . . [Clawson] did that for me, to make sure I knew about it and to make sure I knew how important it was from day one. If she had never spoken up or just figured, "Well, I'll wait for June to ask me more about it," then maybe I wouldn't have, because it was new to me.

During the same group interview, Monterio talked about giving time to Clawson at the faculty meeting to remind staff about the work of the teacher research group, "not letting us forget." She also noted that she was learning more about teacher research and ways to support it by asking the teacher researchers to share ideas with her.

Similarly, Spratley credited the importance of the role of the teacher researcher leader in initiating and sustaining the project.

> While I agree with the notion that principals are important . . . just as important, if not more so, is the selection of the person who brought the concept to the building and who owned it. . . . If teachers are enthusiastic and excited about something it tends to work because they tend to make it work. . . . We are attempting now to have it grow.

Teacher researcher leaders suggested ways for the principal to support the group of teacher researchers such as reading the teacher researchers' articles, dropping in on research meetings, and arranging for roundtable discussions with the staff to share research findings. Teacher researcher leaders also helped to draft correspondence to staff and others outside the school. For example, Clawson helped Monterio send the following message to teachers encouraging them to consider joining the teacher research group:

> As part of our staff development initiative, I want to invite all our faculty to be a part of the Poe Teacher Researcher Team. As you know, Poe is one of only three schools in a grant-funded program to support teacher research in the schools. This offers you an exciting opportunity to explore questions you might have about teaching and learning in your classes. If you are hesitant about doing teacher research, talk to a member of our research team or review some of their studies from the last 2 years. Even if you decide not to conduct research this year, you will hear more about the practical applications of teacher research through Poe's professional development program during the school year.

Principals' Use of Research. Principals helped to support the work of teacher researchers by making connections between teacher researcher knowledge and the school. Spratley stated that he needed to "be creative about ways in which the research can find its way into the places that are meaningful and to be diligent about all of that." He illustrated that idea with an example of how he planned to share with parents at the ninth grade parent orientation a social studies teacher's research on the importance of having ninth graders set and meet goals. The research showed that grades improved—an increase in A's and a decrease in failing grades—when students set goals. Spratley speculated that when he talks with parents of ninth graders who are nervous about their child's performance, sharing the teacher research about the importance of ninth-grade students learning how to develop goals would be very helpful.

SUMMARY OF FINDINGS

The following is a summary of research findings across the two themes discussed in this study and implications as they relate to the role of principals in supporting teacher research in their schools for school improvement.

Principals value the focus that teacher research places on instruction in the school and its impact on student learning, professional development, and the profession. They demonstrated this value by

- Encouraging the use of research findings and research skills of teacher researchers in school planning
- Making connections between the teachers' research findings and instruction in the school
- Supporting the use of time for research meetings
- Providing forums, opportunities, and time for the teacher researchers to share their findings with the school staff

Principals grew to understand teacher research and the impact of teacher research differently. They learned about teacher research as they sought ways to understand and use the process and the results for school improvement based on their vision for their schools. Different emphases emerged such as developing a school culture of inquiry, expanding instructional strategies, making changes in curriculum, and supporting school planning and staff development.

Reciprocal relationships developed between principals and teacher researcher leaders. The relationship that developed between the principal and teacher researcher leader was based on an evolving trust where they gave each other support for implementing the project and support for their differing leadership roles. They each taught the other, speaking from their teacher researcher leader and principal roles and their shared commitment to the project.

Principals recognized the diverse skills of teacher researcher leaders not directly related to their research. Their relationships with teacher researcher leaders enabled principals to learn about the other skills the teachers possessed. Consequently they relied on the leaders to take on different roles or responsibilities in the school, for example, staff developer and school planner.

IMPLICATIONS FOR SCHOOL SYSTEM SUPPORT

The results of this study have implications for school system support for principals and teacher researcher leaders. It is helpful for principals to have an understanding of teacher research and ways to support a teacher research group. In addition, training for teacher researcher leaders that includes working with principals would help schools promote and sustain research communities.

The project provided funds for reassigned time for teacher researcher leaders to perform their various project roles. The time and the project also provided the opportunity for the principal to recognize and tap other skills of the teacher researcher leaders. A question this raises is: How can a school and school district allow for the sharing of leadership roles across teachers and administrators in a school? Reassigned time is one way; other ways need to be explored.

The effects of a group of teacher researchers in a school depend on a variety of factors, not all of which we understand. But clearly, support provided by the principal, although it unfolds differently in different schools, is critical.

CHAPTER 9

Not Entirely by Design: Teacher Research and School Planning

Marion S. MacLean

Schools are complex networks of human interaction.
—James Comer (1980)

During the third year of the teacher research project, Falls Church High School (FCHS) came close to resembling a school in which teachers' individual and collective instructional goals guided the school's 5-year plan. I quickly add two important notes. First, if we came close to reflecting such a school, it was not because we had deliberately worked to reach that goal. Second, readers might think that teachers' instructional goals must guide a school's planning, but often they do not.

Usually school planning is accomplished by small committees who work hard to support efforts in the school that match the district's goals and to meet the district's formal planning requirements—three goals, three work plans, benchmarks, test scores as assessment of success, for instance. To accomplish this task, teachers and administrators on these committees use their best knowledge of the school, but rely mainly on school-level knowledge—not their own individual and collective classroom-based specific and contextual knowledge of student learning in the classrooms at that school. In practice, the emphasis on priorities set beyond the local school level, time and budgetary constraints, and the immediacy of the daily work of schools often undermine the usefulness of the task.

In that last year of the teacher research project, FCHS undertook one new initiative (school renewal) and continued another (block scheduling) in addition to supporting the teacher research group. This chapter follows the three school initiatives—block scheduling, school renewal, and teacher research—over the course of the year, describing ways in which they linked, overlapped, or ran parallel to each other. The block scheduling effort serves as a concrete example of a school initiative monitored by a teacher and staff oversight committee with links through common committee members to both teacher research and school planning. Because I was particularly interested in understanding the possible connections between teachers' research and school planning, I will explain some of the ways in which such connections were effective for school planning and identify characteristics of a school where major links seem to occur efficiently and productively.

The overlapping of members in these groups, the relationships between people in and across groups, the different but connected purposes of the groups, and the limited amount of time during which these groups met— all created a complexity that make it difficult to explain what happened and why. For the sake of clarity, I give descriptions of the groups at first, then explain the overlapping and some of the complexity that played a useful part in fulfilling the school's purposes.

It may sound at times as if the opportunities and links that resulted during this study occurred because we intended them to occur and that we made choices designed to lead us to a conclusion that we anticipated. Although we hoped for such conclusions, we made our choices according to that hope, not because we knew what would result. It is, therefore, remarkable that we arrived at the beginning of that school year facing the possibility of collaborating in ways that were unusual for any school, especially a high school, to experience. We had worked hard to make such collaboration possible, but it had also happened not entirely by design.

THE GROUPS IN PLAY

What follows is a brief description of the groups within the school whose work overlapped and influenced the direction of the school's goals.

The Teacher Research Group

All of us in the FCHS teacher research group that I led were teachers who voluntarily conducted research on our own practices and our own students' learning during the course of the year. We determined our questions based on issues that arose from our classrooms; we used both quantitative and qualitative data; we often enlisted our students' help in conducting the research; and we met regularly to discuss our data and findings. At the end of each year, we published research reports in an in-house publication.

Some of the teachers had continued with the group for more than 1 year (one other teacher and I participated during all 3 years), but most had not. Each year the size of the group varied between six and nine people from different disciplines and with varying degrees of experience in teaching.

The School Planning Group or "Paw Pride"

Falls Church High School's planning group was known as Paw Pride, a name intended to link the school-wide planning effort to school spirit through a reference to our mascot, the Jaguar. Paw Pride consisted of 10 to 15 members representing all of the major departments within the school. It also included two parents and two students (rising seniors). The group's administrative representative, Kelso Delaney, and elected facilitator, Sonya Silberman, prepared for meetings, notified members of upcoming issues and deadlines, and provided leadership for the committee. (Except for the teacher researchers in the project and Lisa Green, I have changed the names of members of the school community.)

This group's purpose was to help the rest of the school identify and articulate the overarching school goals. These were, by district requirement, to take the form of objectives with evaluation components and work plans. The group also had responsibility for monitoring the implementation of work plans, assessing results, revising the plans as needed, and reporting to the school and district on the plan's implementation.

The School Renewal Initiative

To add to Paw Pride's responsibilities, it was again time for FCHS to go through the state accreditation process. Because the state offered an accreditation plan that was similar to the district's plan for setting and achieving goals, our principal gave this group the task of carrying out the "school renewal" option of the accreditation plan. The school renewal process allowed a school to study how it works, assess its effectiveness, and make appropriate changes over a 5-year period in five identified areas:

- School communication
- School climate
- Curriculum and instruction
- Staff development
- School planning

In this way a school could individualize the accreditation process and, in the case of Fairfax County schools, could do so through their school planning groups—while still meeting state requirements.

A Decision Made

A major school committee, the Block Scheduling Oversight Committee, was already addressing important issues related to school renewal. By assessing the school's needs, conducting research, presenting options, adopting a plan, implementing a plan, and preparing to assess the block schedule, this committee had already completed several necessary parts of the school renewal process. Although the block scheduling initiative was not the only vehicle through which we could (or would) accomplish the school renewal goals, that effort was already under way. As a result, Paw Pride members agreed to maintain the issue-based, existing committees.

As a follow-up step, it seemed useful to look at the existing committee organization of the school to determine which was doing what and why. We wanted to duplicate school committees' efforts as little as possible. As is frequently the case in a small high school like ours, one member of the Paw Pride was also a member of the Human Relations Committee—a group that had already taken on the task of naming all of the committees, their memberships, their purposes, and their meeting schedules. Examining existing committee organization was a task that the Human Relations Committee would continue. Other committees, mainly through linking members, would contribute to the creation of a school plan for self-renewal.

The Block Scheduling Oversight Committee

This committee's original purpose was to research different ways of scheduling instructional time, to find out the responses to different schedules in schools that had already adopted them, to present their findings to the faculty and school community for a decision by vote, and to follow up the vote with any needed staff development. The committee was led by Lisa Green, also chair of the English department and an experienced teacher researcher.

As the school prepared to switch from a schedule of seven 50–minute classes each day to four 90–minute classes on alternating days (a "block" schedule), the committee evolved into an oversight committee, a group of nine whose purpose was to monitor the first year of implementation. Green continued as chair, but the group changed much of its membership and prepared to identify schoolwide issues and initiate discussion of possible options and modifications. It was creating and would administer a lengthy faculty survey to collect data that would be the basis for appropriate changes in the block scheduling plans.

The group met at least once a month and had two additional responsibilities:

- collecting and reporting additional data as needed according to expressed faculty concerns
- planning presentations of the findings to the faculty that would allow them to create solutions to the most important issues raised

Although data collection and analysis remained an important part of Paw Pride's role, the Oversight Committee did most of the data collection and analysis for the block scheduling objective during the implementation year.

ONE TEACHER'S RESEARCH

I was interested in the possible connections between school planning and teacher research. It seemed logical that teachers' research might serve as a way to see how block scheduling was working, but how could we do that without overriding individual teachers' decisions about the questions and issues of their own research? Certainly, all of the studies would take place in the context of a blocked schedule, so wouldn't they all in some way contribute to our understanding of the block's impact on instruction? It seemed that it should, but I saw little evidence that we were initially making much use of the links and connections.

I was also intrigued by the connections between and across different groups or committees within the school. As a member of both Paw Pride and the teacher research group, I could examine the ways in which membership on two major committees affected communication within and across those committees, and I could look for ways to promote connections and efficient management of the different groups' purposes.

Three questions, then, gave me direction:

- How does the teacher researcher leader support teachers' research in different ways? In a schoolwide context?
- How do different school groups overlap, and how can we make use of those overlaps, for instance, to unify our purposes and efforts as a school?
- What happens when we *create* overlaps? What strategies and conditions can we initiate that make it likely for people in the school to make cross-group connections?

At the end of the first semester, a review of my notebooks and other data from the beginning of the year disheartened me. I wanted to see evidence of ways in which the three groups overlapped, but overlapping, if it existed, was not apparent. It seemed that groups at FCHS that were implicitly connected did not necessarily develop connections or unify their efforts or even communicate with each other.

The only bit of evidence I had to the contrary was of my own doing. It was a note I had filed—the result of my having asked to be a member of the Block Scheduling Oversight Committee. I believed that it would be sensible for the Block Scheduling Oversight Committee to have a researcher working with it, that my research experience could be of use in helping to carry out the evaluation plan for the block scheduling objective. When the committee chair gave me a note with their response, it read, "Great!" I placed it in one of my folders for ongoing data collection and joined the group.

THE NINTH-GRADE CONNECTION

If useful and efficient connections were going to evolve, it seemed unlikely that they would happen without intervention by people who could see and make use of those potential connections. We would have to work deliberately to establish ways that teacher research and qualitative methodology, for example, could inform school planning and block scheduling. A plan emerged from a familiar source—the academic performance of our ninth graders.

For several years our school plan had acknowledged a need to pay special attention to the academic performance of our ninth-grade students. The objective read that the school would implement plans

> to improve the academic achievement of all students at Falls
> Church H. S. through the implementation of block scheduling with
> special attention to the performance of ninth-grade students.

Ninth Graders and the Block Scheduling Oversight Committee

The Block Scheduling Oversight Committee solicited comments from the faculty throughout the year. In addition, the Oversight Committee administered a midyear survey created by the committee with guidance from the Office of Testing and from me, its new research member. Designed to discover the faculty's adjustment to the new schedule, the survey covered many of the issues about which teachers had expressed the most apprehension. Would students' learning suffer if a class met on Monday and Wednesday but not Tuesday or Thursday? Would more students forget to do homework more frequently? What kinds of activities could usefully fill 90 minutes of instructional time? Several of us tabulated the results and presented them to the whole Oversight Committee in order to plan how to present our findings to the rest of the school.

Those findings indicated that many students were having problems completing their homework with every-other-day classes, and that completing homework on either of the two nights created problems of one sort or another. The faculty and Oversight Committee interpreted these findings to mean that students were having trouble figuring out how to manage time and learning within the framework of the block schedule. For ninth graders, the block schedule seemed to compound the usual adjustment and time-management problems they faced on entering high school.

In addition, the survey also revealed great frustration on the part of teachers and students when students missed a class. Teachers observed that students tended not to check with teachers or with classmates to find out work they had missed, and that missing two classes' worth of instruction as well as major homework assignments resulted in sometimes devastating consequences. Teachers speculated that students had little time to check with their teachers, especially if assignments and class work required much in the way of explanation, and had no scheduled time set aside for making up work missed. Nor did students take responsibility for creating the time and opportunity to do so. Teachers felt that ninth graders, not used to the expectation for taking more responsibility for making up missed work, seemed especially in need of support.

In follow-up sessions with the faculty and staff on the survey results, teachers expressed their belief in a critical need, especially on the ninth-grade level, for students to learn ways to manage their time and their learning. During the last few weeks of school, the faculty created two small groups that would meet during the summer to collect a variety of strategies for both teachers and students to use in addressing these needs. While one of the summer groups would focus on attendance, another would focus on ways that students could manage their own learning better. The faculty asked the groups to present the collections of strategies to the faculty in the workdays before school began in the fall.

Ninth Graders and Teacher Research

Over the 3 years of the grant, teacher researchers' investigations and articles also focused on ninth graders' learning. This emphasis occurred not by design, but by individual teachers' choices.

Year 1

- Bill Plitt wrote about goal setting with ninth graders in his world studies classes.

- Nora Mara wrote about ninth graders' attitudes about school and discovered a plan for teaching writing with them.

Year 2

- Plitt's research on goal setting continued, but branched out to include Michelle Mateka, the learning disabilities teacher who team-taught the world studies classes with him.

Year 3

- Plitt examined the use of art in teaching his world studies ninth graders.
- Mateka examined the use of a student self-evaluation program in her ninth-grade LD basic skills class.
- Lisbeth Strimple examined her use of Silent Sustained Reading with her ninth-grade English students.
- Robert Boyd examined his role in teaching ninth-grade students in his English classes.
- Becky Smith examined ninth graders' strategies for self-evaluation in her earth science classes.
- Lin Spence studied how her ninth-grade "underachieving" students learned in a reading program.

Each year the teacher researchers made their research public to the rest of the school community. We also arranged many occasions during which we involved the rest of the faculty in discussion of our work, and much of our dissemination happened in conversations on hall duty or at the photocopier. In the process, we saw a schoolwide emphasis on ninth graders' learning take shape.

PLAYING TO OUR STRENGTHS

Connections and convergences began to occur. Two of the teachers involved in the summer groups were Curran Roller, a math teacher, and Carrie Perry, an English and journalism teacher who sponsored the school newspaper. These two teachers were also teacher researchers.

Perry, also a member of the Block Scheduling Oversight Committee, facilitated a work session with half of the faculty to determine which needs related to students' learning on the block schedule were most critical. Perry's research reflected an interest in students' and teachers' responsibilities: her article examined ways in which the responsibility for students' listening is a shared one in her classroom.

Roller's work as a teacher researcher focused on project-based learning in mathematics, an approach that revealed issues that arise when a math teacher structures opportunities for students to assume responsibility for their learning.

During the last week of school, as Perry and Roller planned the work of their small summer group, they began searching for articles on self-assessment strategies for students, ways in which students could monitor and assess their own learning. They wanted some examples to present to the other teachers in the summer group since the groups would have little time to compile their own lists of strategies. Perry and Roller had also been interested in an idea expressed during the faculty discussion: that students should assume more responsibility for learning how to learn. If teachers wanted to teach their students how to monitor their own learning, it would help to have these strategies at hand.

Perry and Roller turned to their teacher researcher colleagues for information about where to find good material for the teachers in the summer group. Green, who regularly conducted assessment workshops within and beyond the school, offered her materials. When Roller asked me for information, I gave him volumes of Fairfax County teacher research from a number of years to sift through for articles on helping students assume responsibility for their learning. He and Perry were also able to use the work of their fellow teacher researchers. Several of their colleagues had looked at students' self-assessment, and others had looked at goal setting or self-evaluation.

Like Perry and Roller, several other staff members' interests and circumstances put them in positions to forge links within the school. For example, Donna Manetti, a psychology and sociology teacher, served on the Human Relations Committee. This committee assumed responsibility for communicating to the faculty about the work of the school's many committees and the connections people had to multiple groups. When the need for that information became necessary for the Paw Pride group, Manetti's membership there made it possible for her to link the two separate committees. And, when Manetti offered that information, Silberman and the rest of the group affirmed the Human Relations Committee's responsibility for that information.

In my role as teacher researcher leader, I wanted to serve as a research link and a research resource to the school, someone who might help others at Falls Church High School see the "stuff of school" as data. I thought I might also be able to model ways of looking at data that would help us avoid basing our actions and decisions solely on assumptions. I hoped also that looking at data would promote collaborative efforts to examine, understand, and attempt to solve the problems that we shared. These hopes also reflected my belief that schools need the research skills of teacher researchers as schools plan, assess, and document their progress.

OBSERVATIONS AND TENTATIVE FINDINGS

I arrived at the end of the school year with data about how school governance can capitalize on the strengths within a school and the conditions that make it possible for teachers' classroom and instructional goals to influence a school's planning. In particular, I noted evidence that the presence of teacher research can make specific, valuable contributions to the effectiveness with which a school staff establishes and meets its objectives. This data leads me to suggest the following ideas about school planning, collaboration, and teacher research within a school:

- In order for the planning groups within a school to be productive, those responsible for school planning must have common purposes, and it is helpful for groups responsible for school planning to have members in common. However, having common members and common purposes does not guarantee communication and collaboration among planning groups.
- Faculty members who have membership on several major committees can create connections between and across groups by offering information from other committees' work and discussions. Their success at forging such links is a product both of their willingness and intention to make links and also of the circumstances that put them in a position to create those links.
- In a similar way, when a school, the district, and the state have goals for students' learning that are common to the purposes of classroom teachers, the commonality of the goals may support the achievement of the goals.
- When teacher researchers become part of school planning, they bring research strategies and stances that can be useful in supporting the school's planning process. They can promote a research-based understanding of the school's goals, the school's progress with at least one of those goals, and the school's plans for next steps for those goals.
- When district and state planning requirements for schools are broad enough, schools can set their local, self-identified, specific goals as a first priority, meeting district and state planning requirements as a second priority.

FURTHER QUESTIONS

At Falls Church High School, we orchestrated—only partly by design—the weblike connections described here. A school-based group of teacher researchers with a teacher leader who had released time worked at the core of the school's planning to create conditions that could produce a schoolwide research community. Research findings came to the attention of a particular group within the school—the ninth-grade teachers—and influenced planning for schoolwide programs involving the ninth graders. In addition, the report to the central office documenting the school's progress in meeting its academic objective made use not only of statistical data but also of the data collected through teachers' research studies.

On the one hand, the situation was created through the determination and commitment of teacher researchers who shared what they were learning wherever they had the opportunity to speak—in particular, in the committees on which they served. On the other, it was also created by those of us who had sought membership in school committees, for we took advantage of every opportunity to communicate across groups and to forge common goals.

Looking beyond the Falls Church experience, I wonder what role intentionality plays. Would starting out with the intention to create connections across groups improve school planning, especially if the school included a teacher research group? Or might it take on the character of other burdensome tasks that detract from a school's or teacher's individual goals? Under less favorable conditions, could deliberate choices swing the balance toward success—and, if so, which ones might prove critical to efforts like ours?

As a teacher researcher involved in the process, I report what my data reveals—that at FCHS during this one very busy year, in local and general ways, teacher researchers' efforts to understand the teaching and learning in their own classrooms provided instructional data and instructional direction to the school as a whole.

REFERENCE

Comer, J. (1980). *School power: Implications of an intervention project.* New York: Macmillan.

CHAPTER 10

The Leaven in the Loaf: Teacher Research Knowledge in Schools

Courtney Rogers

It's like the leaven in the loaf—you can't see it working. It starts off
small, but it grows.

—Cheryl Reames

The first time I conducted research in my tenth-grade English classroom, I
was the only teacher researcher in my school. I shared my data and my discoveries with the other teacher researchers in my graduate seminar, and my
research report was eventually published, but what I learned about my students as writers and the effects of my teaching practices on their learning
never made its way beyond my classroom to others in the school.

More than a decade later, my experiences as a teacher researcher, my
work with teacher researcher groups in schools, and the study of an elementary school research group had affirmed for me that teacher research
generates knowledge. It seemed important to ask, What happens to the
knowledge that teacher researchers create? And what are the effects of their
research on their schools?

As I continued to work with the teacher researchers at Lemon Road
School, several other research groups in district schools, teachers and principals in our project, and teacher researcher leaders in the district Teacher
Researcher Network, I added to a growing body of information. I asked
teachers and principals what they saw happening as teachers conducted
research in their schools; I looked for evidence of the ways teacher
researchers' learning made its way into the life of school. My data includes
field notes, tapes and transcriptions, survey and interview results, correspondence and planning documents, and teachers' research reports.

This chapter, then, draws on a wide array of perspectives and includes
the voices of many teachers and principals in our district as they talk about
what happens to teacher researcher knowledge in their schools. The images
and metaphors that emerge from their descriptions suggest an ever widen-
ing circle of growth that begins in a teacher's classroom and moves slowly

and quietly into the school community. Lemon Road Elementary School teacher researcher leader Betsy Sanford uses a similar image as she explains what happened to her research learning:

> My research on number facts with last year's [first-grade] class led to some rethinking about the relationship of number facts to problem solving and mental math, and that research has begun to have a ripple effect in our school.

Fellow teacher researcher Rekha Patel suggested to Sanford and her colleagues that their research was first helping them in their classrooms, and "then it creeps out to others." The images suggest a slow and steady movement similar to that offered by Cheryl Reames—"the leaven in the loaf."

Beginning with teachers discussing their classroom research with each other, I will describe what I learned about the movement of research knowledge as it rises, expands, creeps, and ripples outward from their classrooms and into their school communities.

TEACHER TALK ABOUT CHANGES IN PRACTICE

The effects of teachers' research knowledge are first made public in their dialogue with research colleagues. "I don't know what I would have done if I'd had this class my first year teaching photography," high school art teacher, Olene Albertson remarked to her research group. She appreciated the opportunity for talk and the support of her colleagues as she documented a difficult year with students who resisted many of the assignments and strategies that had worked well with her previous students. She described the research practice of observing and writing about her students as "the best thing I have ever done as a teacher." Her research led her to a recognition: "I didn't need to teach the way I used to." Albertson described as the "turning point" in the year her decision to "throw out the textbook," "listen to . . . what [students] want to do," and "take risks" as she began to involve students in the planning of instruction.

As the year and her research progressed, Albertson shared her discoveries with her colleagues. The students who were such a handful to manage in the classroom were producing "high-level work" comparable to work produced by her outstanding students the previous year. The key, she observed, was that these "students share in the directions we go in." When another teacher in the research group asked, "Would you take what you have learned from this difficult group and apply it to any photography class?" Albertson answered that she would indeed: "All kids need input" into the class curriculum.

Teacher researchers learn from and with one another. I have heard teacher researchers thank each other for the learning that came out of their research meetings, for nudging them to rethink an aspect of their teaching or see an element in their classroom in a different light, and for spurring them on to attempt a new strategy or adapt a lesson plan based on their colleague's research. Much of the change prompted by teachers' research occurs when teachers work together in what one teacher researcher described as "informal staff development."

CHANGES IN COLLEAGUES' TEACHING

Research leader Marion MacLean spoke about the influence of individual teacher researchers at Falls Church High School on their department colleagues. A math teacher who studied the effects of project-based learning with his students initiated conversations with other math teachers that got them "interested in what he is doing and trying things that he's done." A science teacher who conducted research on learning groups influenced her department chair to use groups in the teaching of chemistry and encouraged a new teacher in the science department to participate in the research group.

MacLean noted that her research colleagues "remark on this being a different kind of talking about teaching and learning—different from those very practical, pragmatic problem-solving kinds of conversations" about classroom life. As she explained,

> The nature of the . . . teacher research work is really to do a lot more than just solve problems. It is to understand what's going on [in our classroom] at its most basic level. . . . What does this look like or how can we understand what this is in order to approach it most effectively for our students' learning?

The kind of sharing that influences a colleague's teaching can be a delicate dance. At a research group meeting in an elementary school, teachers discussed ways to communicate to colleagues both the value of conducting research and the implications of their research for other classrooms in the school. With the encouragement of her principal and teacher colleagues, teacher Margie Henry had studied the use of language arts portfolios with her first and second graders. Using portfolios to look closely and regularly at her students' work resulted in what she described as "a shift" in her teaching to "instructional planning based on daily assessment of children."

As Henry and her group talked about communicating the implications of their research to colleagues beyond the research group, both Henry and kindergarten teacher Cheryl Reames expressed concern that teachers might perceive the sharing as prescriptive. Henry was uncomfortable about the prospect that teachers might interpret her message as: "What I'm doing is the example and you should be doing this."

Reames noted a similar discomfort about sharing her research and being seen as assuming the role of "expert." She recognized that the effects of their work would take time and imagined the course of teacher research in a school: "It's like the leaven in the loaf—you can't see it working. It starts off small, but it grows."

The comments of the teacher researchers illustrate some of the complexity and difficulty of integrating teacher research knowledge into the fabric of teaching and learning in the school. Teachers may lack confidence in their own research findings or doubt the desire of their colleagues to learn from them.

GENERATING AND EVALUATING PROGRAMS

Kathy Hermann, leader of a research group in her high school, conducted research with her ESOL students that revealed their frustration over stereo-typed impressions of them and their countries. This discovery eventually led to the design and implementation of a new program—an annual Heritage Day that involved the entire school community in celebrating the diverse cultures in the school. Hermann said of conducting research:

> What I like best is the surprise element that inevitably crops up— something that had never occurred to me before. And if I didn't have this data to look at, it would have gone right by me. It would have just slipped completely away if I hadn't been systematically looking at it.

Hermann knows that the learning from classroom research can lead to the creation of new programs to meet the particular learning needs of students in a school. She explained what she had noticed about the relation of teachers' individual research questions to programs in her school:

> Sometimes the idea for questioning something comes directly from the teacher and her experience in the classroom . . . or

sometimes, if a program is mandated, you think, "Well, is this really a good way?" . . . A teacher researcher can systematically look at it . . . and then have some idea of whether it really works or doesn't.

Hermann views the systematic collection and analysis of research data as a way of examining programs to evaluate their effectiveness as well as adapt or revise them. One year, while teachers at her high school developed a conflict mediation program, Hermann conducted research with her ESOL students on the effects of learning mediation skills as they learned English. While Hermann gained insights that informed her teaching, her research also contributed to her colleagues' understanding of the school-wide effort to teach students to resolve conflicts peacefully.

PROFESSIONAL DEVELOPMENT

Teacher researchers at Lemon Road came to view their research as self-directed professional development. Vicki Ellison saw her research as

one of the best ways for me to grow professionally because a lot of the inservices . . . that we have to go to don't seem that important or relevant to me. This gives me that opportunity to really look at what I want to look at and to explore things that I think I need to know more about.

Her colleague, Shannon Frigon, described research as "the space where you make sense of things."

Teachers' research can also shape the school's staff development. Principal Carolyn Williams explained her sense of the effect of Vicki Ellison's research on spelling with her Grade 2/3 students:

When we first started the research project our spelling programs were very traditional . . . teachers giving the words and every Friday [students] tested on the words and then they're never seen again. . . . Since that time [other teachers] adopted [Ellison's] program and now they're using it with the Grade 4/5/6 kids, selecting their own spelling words . . . in a more thoughtful way.

Sanford explained how her math research informed her role as math lead teacher, responsible for coordinating staff development in her school:

> As math lead teacher at Lemon Road, I work with other teachers.
> . . . I share strategies, resources, and my current thinking about
> math. It is an opportunity for dialogue about math.

Two and a half years into the teacher researcher project at Falls Church High School, principal Marvin Spratley noted the tremendous potential he saw for a teacher—"whether a strong teacher or otherwise"—to learn from teacher researcher colleagues. In contrast to "distant research findings," teacher researcher learning is "immediate and it's at home; you're not reading through the literature for it." He expressed disappointment that he had not seen more teachers drawn into the collegial dialogue, expanding the sphere of influence: "There seems to be a nucleus of thoughtful people, . . . a next level out who touch base from time to time to benefit or engage in conversation, then those who are out[side]" the circle.

For a teacher researcher group to support professional growth that has impact on a school as a whole, it must continue from year to year. In schools that have maintained a group, some teachers take part yearly as it becomes a way of teaching and growing for them, while others participate as their interests and lives permit.

RESEARCH SKILLS AND SCHOOL DECISION MAKING

Teachers' research skills begin to be recognized as valuable beyond their classrooms. Falls Church High School research leader MacLean talked about faculty perceptions: "People around the building see me as a researcher and I think they see the other people in the [research] group as researchers as well." These perceptions account in part for MacLean's role in assessing the school's new block scheduling structure as the staff sought to make it work. She led the design and implementation of a staff survey, the collection and analysis of the data, and the dissemination of the results to the staff.

Some of the survey data was highly charged, reflecting tension created by the diverse perspectives of faculty members. MacLean drew on her research knowledge and skills to "point out the ways in which people's [survey] comments could be turned into questions that might lead us toward an understanding of the issue or a kind of 'let's find out' position." She helped colleagues view the data systematically and dispassionately. MacLean explained:

> Parts of the research stance and methodology contribute to the
> kinds of attitudes or assumptions . . . that forge the ability to work

together rather than to see each other in different camps. . . . It's almost like what you do in mediation: You ask a question together, and the question then becomes the responsibility of all parties to solve, to address, explore, find out more about. It's not adversarial.

Hermann, too, noted the value of research skills to her collaboration with colleagues:

Respect for other people's points of view . . . is a skill that people need on planning teams. . . . On a research team you get to look at somebody else's thought processes . . . and see how they came to a certain point. Once you do that for a while, you have more respect for people who think differently because you see how people get from the data to their conclusion. It's actually a pretty life-changing thing.

Both MacLean and Hermann see research experience and skills as contributing to effective collaboration and data-based decision making at their schools.

TEACHER RESEARCH AND SCHOOL PLANNING

For a number of years my colleague Mary Ann Nocerino and I had supported school teams of teacher leaders and their principals in a collaborative planning and evaluation process aimed at improving student achievement. They assessed the learning needs of their students based on a variety of data about them and their achievement, developed schoolwide objectives and implemented plans to address those needs, and collected ongoing data to evaluate the results of their efforts.

Nocerino and I knew from our work in schools with effective planning teams and teacher researcher groups that, where both existed, teachers' research data and findings often provided information about student learning in their classrooms that had important connections to the needs of students across the school and to schoolwide instructional priorities. What some teacher researchers were learning from classroom inquiry could add clarity and depth to their school's responses to questions about how students were achieving and help them move on to questions about what they as a staff might do to improve their students' learning.

At a seminar sponsored by the Teacher Researcher Network, an elementary school principal talked about the benefits of having both a teacher research group and a collaborative planning team in her school. She observed that "the teacher research group studying instruction expands classroom walls" as teachers often invite each other into their classrooms, while the planning team helps provide a "broader perspective" that keeps staff "informed about the whole school." She stated that "teacher research has helped sustain innovation and school reform."

Hermann believes that a number of things have contributed to meaningful links between the teacher research and school planning teams in her school. From the beginning "both the teacher research group and the planning group . . . were interested in finding out more about how students learn and making the learning environment better for the teachers and the students." Neither group was "defined along department lines;" both were looking at schoolwide issues. At the same time, "several people in our teacher researcher group were finding needs in our classrooms that turned out to be needs that the whole school had as well."

Hermann talked about the "constant cross-fertilization" that occurred when she and colleague teacher researchers were also serving on the school planning team. "When there are teacher researchers on the planning committee . . . there is generally a voluntary exchange of ideas." As Hermann and other planning team members were looking at how they could acknowledge cultural diversity in the school, she was conducting research with her ESOL students. It was the findings from this classroom research that made their way to the school planning committee and helped shape the school's Heritage Day.

Hermann's continued work with her students revealed that an annual cultural event was not enough. "You can't just do this on one day, Mrs. Hermann!" her students told her. As a result, she began to plan joint instruction with other teachers that involved ongoing interaction between her students and other students in the school. She also worked with students and staff to involve ESOL students in leadership positions in student government.

Hermann talked about something else that she saw as contributing to the connections:

> I was not as involved in my school before I became a teacher
> researcher. . . . There was a certain confidence that I was able to
> get from knowing that I knew how to collect data, I knew how to
> analyze data, I knew how to share it with people. I was excited
> about what I was doing in my class. I really wanted to be able to
> share that with people. People on the teacher research team did
> get involved with the planning group because, once we had this
> knowledge, we wanted to be able to make a difference in our
> building.

Sanford's remarks echo Hermann's experience: "As I became more confident about my math research, I became more confident about my math lead role in the school." She explained:

> Because of the math research I've done over the past two and a half years, I have rethought math objectives. I would like to influence our planning about math schoolwide, so that there is a greater emphasis on mental math, number facts, and problem solving, and so that we see those areas of math instruction intertwined.

Sanford also talked about the collective effects on the school of the research conducted by teachers over two and a half years:

> The program at Lemon Road is beginning to benefit from the hard look we've taken in a collaborative setting at instructional issues. Not one of us has all the answers—although our research has certainly produced some—but together we have a way to search for answers.

In the school's third year with a research group, several of the teacher researchers served on the leadership team that developed a schoolwide objective on inquiry as the basis for teacher and student learning. The rationale for the school plan objective noted that the experience of teacher researchers at the school over 3 years suggests that "meaningful learning for teachers comes from choosing an area to examine and having the support of other teachers during the course of that exploration."

At both Sanford's and Hermann's schools, teacher researchers' participation as school planning team members resulted in the useful exchange of information for school planning and evaluation.

SUSTAINING THE GROWTH

The coexistence in a school of a teacher research group and a planning process that involves teachers does not guarantee, as MacLean notes, that connections between the two will occur or that research knowledge will inform decision making (see also Chapter 9). The linking is largely dependent on teacher researchers' willingness to invest their time and energy in both classroom research and school planning at the same time they carry out the responsibilities of teaching their students. Without (and even with) overlapping of roles, Hermann sees the need for both researchers and planners to communicate and collaborate. Researchers need to share their findings and school planners need to pay attention to them.

The role of a teacher who provides leadership for the research group over time is critical (see Chapter 11). Hermann, leader for most of the 7 years the research group has continued at her school, sees teacher research as "an agent for change" but observes that the change may not occur in predictable ways. She cited the difficulties of sustaining a group in the school: "There does have to be somebody who is willing to take the responsibility to make sure that things move along. And sometimes it is very difficult."

MacLean observed that conducting classroom research and participating in a research group is "hard, demanding, and rigorous" as well as "rewarding" and does not automatically "flourish" or grow "in a very increasingly large circle."

Growth may be fragile, gradual, visible only now and then, slow to develop and difficult to sustain. As one teacher researcher observed, "Development of school impact doesn't happen the first year. It begins to happen in subsequent years as teacher researchers see that it can have implications for the school. In dialogue with other teacher researchers [we] begin to see implications—that's when you get the school plan piece."

Sanford speculates on what may contribute to the time it takes:

> It seems to me, thinking through the kind of impact that teacher research is having at Lemon Road, that it takes a few years of a teacher being involved in research before that teacher's research moves beyond his or her classroom. That may be because it takes that long for most researchers to have confidence in what they are learning and the way they are learning it; it may be because it takes a long time to solidify what one learns. . . . Some of the research from the Lemon Road group, while important [to the school], is still playing its biggest role in those teachers' own teaching.

MacLean agrees that for now the greatest impact of teacher research on her school is evident in teachers' classrooms: "I have no doubt that there has been some effect in terms of student achievement . . . but to see that, you have to look at our individual classrooms, at our work as teachers."

FINDINGS AND CONCLUSIONS

This study provides an emerging description of what happens to teachers' research knowledge in a school and its impact over time on the teaching and learning that go on there. The effects of this knowledge become evident as teachers gain confidence in its worth and it makes its way into the conversations and work of other teachers and administrators in the school. A summary of the findings of my study follows this expansion process.

- The effects of teachers' research knowledge are first evident in their dialogue with teacher researcher colleagues and then in the teaching of their colleagues.
- Teachers' research generates new programs and contributes to thoughtful implementation and ongoing assessment of existing programs.
- Teacher researchers direct their individual and collective professional development in a school.
- Teacher researchers develop skills that enhance a school's capacity for data-based decision making and professional collaborations.
- Teacher researcher leaders, with the support of their principals, can forge meaningful connections between teacher research and school planning.

In a school over time teacher research can help to create a climate of professional commitment through collegial support and a systematic way of generating knowledge about teaching and learning. While the impact of teacher research in a school emerges gradually and grows slowly, recalling the images of ripples in a pond and leaven in a loaf, its strength and staying power come from its origins—the discoveries of teacher researchers and their students in the classrooms of the school.

CHAPTER 11

Teacher Researcher Leadership

Mary Ann Nocerino

A leader is a leader when others follow. I'm following but I am next to her.

—a member of a teacher research group

My interest in teacher leadership began when I was assigned to a school as a reading teacher after 7 years of classroom experience. At the time the role of the reading teacher was changing from a teacher with responsibility for small groups of children having difficulty learning to read to responsibility for the entire school reading program, including staff development in reading. I knew of no models for this change and it presented a challenge to both my existing role as teacher and my professional relationship with my peers. The tension I felt could best be stated by the question a colleague asked me: "How can one of the sheep be a leader of the fold?"

I saw myself as a teacher, yet I was conducting staff development and shaping school policy in reading—tasks that teachers don't typically perform. Later, my work with teachers and administrators involved providing support for groups of teacher researchers and for teams developing and implementing school plans. Teachers who are involved in these activities often assume leadership responsibilities as they work to improve the student achievement in their schools.

But even though there have been some changes in the role of teachers, teaching is still a very private activity often characterized by autonomy and isolation. For teaching and learning to improve it is my assumption that teachers must play more of a leadership role in their schools. Schools have not nurtured their most important resource—their teachers. Not only has teacher leadership not been fostered, the culture in education works counter to it.

The teacher researcher project provided me with an opportunity to study teacher leadership. The elementary, middle, and high schools each had an experienced teacher researcher leading the research group at her school as well as coleading the project. Their participation in the project led to roles and responsibilities for them that were not typical for classroom teachers. These included overall planning for the project, creating a network for teacher researchers in the school system, providing staff development for administrators and teachers about teacher research, and leading a group of teacher researchers in their schools. In addition, the three teacher researcher leaders conducted research on their own teaching and student learning.

To carry out these responsibilities two of five teaching periods were allocated to project activities for the middle and high school teachers. A full-time instructional aide was assigned to the elementary teacher to provide her with time and flexibility.

DATA COLLECTION

In my role as a member of the Planning Group, the high school teacher research group, and central office staff, I collected the following data on teacher leadership:

- A research log of notes and reflections about such project activities as planning meetings, school group meetings and workshops
- Notes from conversations with many of the teacher researchers in the three project schools
- Written responses from teacher researchers in the three project schools to the following prompt: Describe a person who you think is a teacher leader. What makes you think of this person as a teacher leader? What are qualities of teacher leadership?
- Taped and transcribed interviews with the three teacher researcher leaders asking how they became teacher leaders, their perception of teacher leadership, and their perceptions of their leadership role in the project

This data allowed me to see themes related to how teacher researcher leaders operated and how their roles were defined by others as well as by themselves. In this chapter the three teacher researcher leaders—Betsy Sanford, Sheila Clawson, and Marion MacLean—are referred to by their real names, but the other teacher researchers are referred to by pseudonyms in order to maintain their anonymity.

The data for this study yields insight into the specific ways that teacher researcher leadership is shaped and how it is viewed by both the leaders and their colleagues. A picture of leadership emerges that is neither conventional nor simple.

TEACHER RESEARCHER LEADERS PLAY MULTIPLE ROLES

The teacher researcher leaders play multiple roles, sometimes all at once, in which they collaborate as peers and leaders, conduct research, and facilitate the learning of their peers and students. Historically, few of these roles existed for teachers. They were "insiders" because they were teachers, yet they were "outsiders" because their new roles required different behaviors and responsibilities outside of the traditional role of teaching. How does a teacher researcher leader identify and carry out these roles?

To act in any role other than a peer or to have a smaller teaching load has the potential to set teacher researcher leaders apart from other teachers in a way that could negatively influence their work. Indeed, in response to the leadership prompt two teacher researchers commented that a teacher leader should not have a reduced teaching load, less time with students, or advanced placement students exclusively. And a high school teacher not involved with the project commented that she knew a teacher who "ruined her reputation" when she accepted a modified teacher schedule to coordinate a program at her school. A differentiated role can be a hazard for teacher leaders in the present culture of schools. Because the teacher researcher leaders had differentiated roles and reduced teaching responsibilities, they had to handle some of the real or imagined tensions associated with these changes.

A Teacher Who Leads and Follows

When I asked the teacher researchers to write about teacher leadership, many described teacher leadership in ways not associated with the traditional notions of leadership. They contrasted typical hierarchical or authoritarian characteristics of leadership with other characteristics. One teacher wrote that a teacher leader "needs to be a good follower [as well as] . . . lead in a traditional way." Another wrote that a teacher leader "is an authority but not authoritarian." Several teacher researchers wrote that they expected teacher leaders to describe their shortcomings as well as the successes of their classroom experiences. Teacher leaders invite others into their classrooms and seek feedback about what they have seen. These teacher researchers expect a teacher leader to be a colleague first, an insider, one who is dealing with the same issues and challenges. Credibility is based on this shared experience.

The teacher researcher leaders are aware of the importance of credibility when balancing the tension of being an insider and outsider. MacLean, teacher researcher leader at the high school, comments: "sometimes you have to let go a little to maintain credibility . . . like voice some judgments that are not the kind a researcher would make such as, 'These kids can't learn this vocabulary.'" A researcher would ask questions to try to figure out what kind of problem the students were having and what might be causing the difficulty, such as, Which words did the kids have problems with? Is there a pattern? MacLean's fudging in her judgment statement illustrated an attempt to straddle the insider and outsider roles. Teacher leadership is "like membership in a club. In order to be a leader you have to be a member of the club."

Leadership as it is described above is laced with collaborative and collegial elements. Perhaps, as MacLean offered, these elements help to soften the alienating nature or outsider role of leadership. Teacher researcher leaders value collaborative decision making as well as a strong commitment to the profession. Sanford, teacher researcher leader at the elementary school, commented:

> I think teacher leaders are passionate about teaching, kids, and learning. I don't see them as people who seek positions with titles, but when you have a teacher who has a strong, not abrasive, voice who is willing to work hard for kids . . . [it] tends to be a unifying voice.

Sanford went on to provide an example of what she meant:

> I guess the picture I have is somebody like [teacher researcher] Yeshe. Whenever she has an idea that may be good [for the school], she always presents it as, "How does this sound to you?" . . . Yeshe was coordinating International Night . . . [sharing] the plans about a map where kids would indicate where they born. . . . One of the teachers said, "You know there are some families who don't know where they were are from." . . . Yeshe asked, "Do you think this is something we should not do?" She was so open to that.

Yeshe demonstrated responsiveness to her colleague's thinking and a willingness to change plans.

A Teacher Who Is a Peer Researcher

During a meeting of the research group in her school, MacLean asked the six teacher researchers to list a finding and then write an implication of the finding for teaching. This was the first meeting focused on findings and implications. After some time for writing, the teachers tentatively shared aloud their attempts. MacLean and the teachers asked questions to help clarify some of the responses. After most of the teacher researchers in the group shared, MacLean started to read her finding and implication to the group but deviated from her written response when she realized her thinking was unclear. Some of the other teacher researchers tried to help her think through her finding and implication by asking questions and rephrasing some ideas, much as MacLean had modeled earlier.

Directly after MacLean's attempt, Naomi volunteered to read her finding and implication. Some time after the meeting, MacLean related a follow-up conversation she had had with Naomi. "When I made that botched attempt at stating a finding and an implication, Naomi said that it was then that she felt she could share."

Another teacher offered some insight into this response and the role of teacher leadership during an all-day work session. She commented:

> I see her [MacLean] as vulnerable, as I am vulnerable as a researcher. If I don't know all the answers, I feel vulnerable. Her saying, "I don't know the answer, I don't know what to do next in my research," gives me permission.

Expression of vulnerability is typical of an insider, one who trusts her colleagues and whose colleagues trust her, and vulnerability is one aspect of being a peer researcher as well as a peer teacher.

A Teacher Who Is a Facilitator of Learning

When teacher researcher leaders describe their teaching role with both students and colleagues, they describe themselves as facilitators helping others figure out what they need to know. In an interview, Sanford illustrated this role when working with her colleague Lisa:

> The one thing I agonize over, and it's tough in the teacher researcher leader role, is intervention—where is that little place where I might do or say or model something that helps somebody else make a leap without making it become my learning instead of her learning. . . . When intervention is heavy handed it stops being Lisa's learning and . . . becomes a puzzle I am figuring out. . . . A good teacher researcher leader is figuring out what Lisa might need.

Figuring out what Lisa might need requires that Sanford listen carefully so she can help Lisa make connections in her thinking. However, knowing how and when to intervene is based on being able to "hear" when listening. One struggling novice teacher researcher leader said, "I wish I could hear things the way she [Sanford] does." Asking the right questions, modeling what needs to be modeled, and providing the appropriate information to facilitate the learning of others require that teacher researcher leaders are knowledgeable and adept in their practice. When asked to reflect on teacher leadership, MacLean responded:

> This is tricky . . . people who have been most influential to me are leaders who are accomplished teachers of the subject who never presumed they knew the answers about what should be happening in my classroom.

The several roles of the teacher researcher leaders are played with different intensity depending on the situation, but the roles coexist. For example, Sanford talked about a conversation she had with a colleague who raised a research issue related to Sanford's former student. Sanford had to weigh two of her roles and perspectives, that of teacher researcher leader and that of a colleague who previously worked with the student and had her own assessment of the student. As a colleague, Sanford said she might tell the teacher her assessment of the student, for example, "I think he has a visual processing problem." In her teacher researcher leader role, she might ask, "Have you ever wondered about his visual processing?" trying to bring into focus for her colleague something she thought might be significant without being prescriptive. "I'm not sure that my interpretation would be valuable or correct. To the extent I give her my thinking, I don't show respect for her thinking and judgment."

While teacher researcher leaders have different roles that require that they be both members of the group and outsiders, there are some characteristics of their leadership that cut across the roles.

CHARACTERISTICS OF TEACHER RESEARCHER LEADERSHIP

As teacher researcher leaders worked out their roles, characteristics emerged, such as teaching, researching, and learning in public; flexibility and willingness to provide leadership in nonrelated activities; and continued examination of their theories.

Teaching, Researching, and Learning in Public

The teacher researcher leaders see themselves as learners who are curious about the many facets of teaching and student learning and who use their research to learn. Despite the many frustrations of teaching, teacher researcher leaders are excited about their own learning and their struggle with the many dilemmas of teaching.

One teacher researcher viewed teacher leaders as learners who share their work with their colleagues:

> Teacher leaders question and wonder. They share their observations and look to find more (questions, observations, wonder, and so on). Generally teacher leaders look and go beyond.

In response to the interview questions, How did you become an education leader? What were some of the influences on you? Clawson, replied that it was her zest for learning that started at the beginning of her teaching over 27 years ago.

> I kept wanting to learn . . . and if someone was paying me to go for training I was expected to share. I was always willing to share. . . . I like to share what I'm enthusiastic about.

Clawson was also willing to take on what other people would not. For example, early in her career she was offered a combination fourth-, fifth-, and sixth-grade gifted and talented class. She said, "No one else wanted to touch it." No one had training in gifted education at the time. Clawson agreed to teach it with the understanding that she could teach it the way she wanted. Later, she became part of the first group in the district receiving training in gifted education. She then provided workshops for other teachers. This was a pattern repeated throughout her career.

In our interview, MacLean responded to the question about her history as a leader as follows:

> I didn't set out to be a "leader." In fact, I think I've taken on "leadership" roles pretty much with the attitude that it's important to support teachers in their teaching and learning, not to suggest what teachers should do. I use myself and my own experience as a learner. . . . I think in some way that has made it possible for me to achieve a position of leadership.

My interviews confirmed that teacher researcher leaders need and value their own learning and also revealed the extent to which they will go to satisfy that need. When I asked teacher researchers in the three schools to define teacher leadership, several teachers also commented on this characteristic. One wrote the following:

A person I think is a teacher leader actually is the leader of our teacher research group. What makes her a leader, in my mind, is her willingness (overwhelming desire?) to seek solutions. She's the kind of person you want to go to talk to about a problem you're having because instead of trying to top it with one of her own problems (in which case you get involved in an infamous teacher gripe session), she suddenly takes it on as a new riddle to solve.

Not that it becomes her problem, but it becomes part of the whole of teaching and learning philosophy, a question that follows from and builds on other questions she has or others have. . . . If a good teacher is someone who models learning, making connections, asking her students more questions, a teacher leader is someone who models learning about teaching to other teachers.

Other teacher researchers described teacher leaders as willing to take risks, solve challenging problems, and seek renewal through formal staff development, education courses, or informal writing activities. They were seen as teachers who continue to educate themselves, read research, question, and scrutinize their techniques.

Teacher researcher leaders are learners who make their teaching and learning public through their research groups and their conversations with other educators, and by inviting others into their classrooms and teaching in others' classrooms. Each of the three teacher researcher leaders in this project has published articles about their teaching and research, another way they make their thinking and practice public.

Flexibility and Responsibility Beyond the Project

Because of their leadership positions in their schools, teacher researcher leaders found themselves assuming roles and responsibilities not anticipated. These included providing workshops to staff at their schools in areas of their expertise but not defined by the project, coteaching, training instructional assistants, and mentoring new teachers. Some of these additional staff development aspects of their roles had both positive and negative sides as explained by two of the teacher leaders.

Sanford provided training for her full-time instructional assistant so that she could carry on with the instructional program when Sanford was involved in project activities. Sanford also had to write more detailed lesson plans so that her instructional assistant could easily carry them out. Although all this took additional time, Sanford felt she and her students benefited from having another competent and trained educator in the classroom.

Teaming at the middle school is structured so that each team includes a subject area teacher for English, math, science, and social studies. The teachers all share the same students and plan the instructional program together. Because of the teaming at middle school, Clawson devoted time to working with the teacher who taught the two classes normally assigned to Clawson.

> My planning time with my coteacher has increased. She is a
> teacher researcher and coteacher on the same middle school team.
> . . . It's important to plan together because we need some consis-
> tency on the team and sometimes she takes over my classes. This
> is her first year in the school system. . . . [It's been a] wonderful
> experience and opportunity for her . . . she is benefiting a lot and
> the team benefits from her work across the disciplines.

In addition, Clawson observes her coteacher and provides feedback on her teaching. She enjoys her mentor role.

The teacher researcher leader role spills over into other areas of the school. Sanford conducted a workshop in teaching math and Clawson organized a faculty meeting with two other teacher researchers on portfolio assessment. MacLean was invited to coteach in a teacher researcher's classroom.

Due to space limitations at her school and her reduced number of scheduled classes, MacLean lost her classroom space, which made great demands on her flexibility. She shared rooms with three other teachers and kept her teaching materials on a cart that she moved from one teaching space to another. MacLean felt that moving from space to space made her more visible and also may have gained her some empathy from her colleagues. Although the situation was barely workable, the space dilemma emphasized the collegial nature of her leadership role and did not place MacLean in a special status of receiving privileges.

Articulating, Revising, and Exploring Theory

The three teacher researcher leaders, with an average of over 25 years of teaching experience, routinely examine their assumptions about teaching and learning. Far from thinking they have figured out how to teach, they are constantly searching for ways to build on their experience and knowledge. MacLean explains:

> I think leadership does not come from a body of knowledge. That's
> not the source. Maybe it comes from asking questions about the

relationship between the big issues and my own classroom and constantly trying to juggle. I can't do that for anybody [else]. I think that part of what makes it possible for me to be viewed as a leader is that I don't offer answers for others. I share my experience, but I don't presume to have the answers for others.

Teacher researcher leaders continually explore the relationships among their theories, their practice, and their reading. This characteristic provides a foundation for their leadership and credibility among their peers.

Carving out time for reflection and learning is a challenge. Some examples follow to illustrate a few of the ways that the teacher researcher leaders manage to find some precious time. In the early morning hours, before reporting to work, Sanford finds quiet time to write and reflect in her teaching log to figure out how her students learn math, her current area of research. MacLean jots down observations and notes in her research journal during class. Sometimes she closes her classroom door at the end of the day to reflect and write in her journal. Clawson gives her classes a few minutes of reflection time at the end of the class period through activities such as asking students to write a question or one thing they learned. She uses this time to write quick notes to capture thoughts, which she elaborates on in more quiet moments.

In my interview with Sanford she commented that leaders are grounded in their teaching because they know what they think. One of her formative experiences was taking a graduate theory course in which, in addition to course readings, she had to write her theory of teaching and learning. She commented that she thinks it might be difficult for teachers to be leaders early in their careers because part of leadership is being in a school and knowing the reality of school life. Teacher leaders take that knowledge and systematically reflect on their classroom and school.

This characteristic is perhaps best summed up by a teacher researcher who described a teacher leader as one who is a "good thinker who also helps those around her become good thinkers too and maybe see things differently or in a new light."

SUMMARY AND CONCLUSION

Built into the project were time and school system supports for the three teacher researcher leaders to colead project activities and lead school-based teacher research groups. Both time and support enabled teacher leadership to unfold and in many ways it has developed a look of its own. The teacher researcher leaders straddle the "insider" role of teacher and the "outsider" role of leader. They have expanded the notion of leadership, and in the process they are helping to change the role of teachers.

It is important to recognize the roles and the characteristics of teacher leadership so they can be nurtured and supported.

- Teacher researcher leaders play multiple roles. They are teachers who lead and follow. They are peer researchers who facilitate the learning of others. They lead by asking questions, at times exposing their uncertainty and vulnerability, characteristics often not associated with leadership.
- Teacher researcher leaders teach, research, and learn in public. They prize learning and model their learning for others. They teach in colleagues' classrooms and invite others into their classrooms.
- Teacher researcher leaders are flexible and provide leadership in areas not defined by project role. They are involved in the school and provide staff development for their colleagues.
- Teacher researcher leaders articulate their theories about teaching and learning, which they continue to explore and revise. They are grounded in theory and the practice of teaching.

The teacher researcher leaders may not have begun their careers with an agenda to become leaders; however, their desire, drive, and need to figure out how their students learn and how best to teach were factors that contributed to their leadership positions. In *On Leadership* (1990), James Gardner stresses that leadership should not be confused with status or power. The teacher researcher leaders in the project do not have official authority, title, or power, but they have influence. Their influence is encapsulated in the following quote from a teacher researcher regarding the teacher research leader of her school research group: "A leader is a leader when others follow. I'm following, but I am next to her."

REFERENCE

Gardner, J. (1990). *On leadership*. New York: Free Press.

CHAPTER 12

The Teacher Researcher Network

Courtney Rogers

> The colleague-to-colleague talk, the dialogue, must continue. That is
> what brings us to the table.
> —Teacher Researcher Network meeting notes

It is after school and the sun is already on its way down on a February afternoon outside a high school classroom. Inside, seated in student desks,
munching on pretzels and grapes, a group talks animatedly about the regional teacher researcher conference they are planning for the spring. They discuss workshops to be offered and selections for the panel of teachers who
will share their recent research on parent involvement. They agree that the
roundtables featuring teachers reporting on their classroom research and
involving participants in discussion are the heart of the conference. "The col-
league-to-colleague talk, the dialogue, must continue. This is what brings us
to the table and makes us come back for more," the meeting notes will later
summarize. The planning goes on intently for well over an hour.

A few teachers leave and others arrive and arrange snacks on their paper
plates, as the second half of the meeting gets under way. For the first few
minutes, everyone writes silently in response to one member's request for
data she is gathering on the group's activities. She wants to know what they
see as the role of the group and how they view their participation in it.

The brief, subdued discussion that follows is in marked contrast to the
energy and excitement of the earlier conference planning. One member
comments on the "strange shifts" that occur in the work of the group, from
dialogue with a colleague in support of her research, for example, to political strategizing within a huge bureaucracy. Others share their weariness
and disappointment over what they perceive as lack of support for the
work of teacher researchers in their school system. Noting the agenda items
remaining, the meeting facilitator shifts the focus to suggestions for updat-
ing the group's Web site.

Next, they talk with renewed resolve about an upcoming meeting with
school district administrators to request support for teacher research. One
member distributes copies of proposed documents to be included in a pack-

et of supporting materials, and her colleagues suggest deletions, additions, and changes. A proposal outlining the kinds of support requested is discussed and revisions offered. Finally, as the meeting is adjourned a few minutes after 7:00, one teacher agrees to respond to a request from a nearby university professor; she will somehow find time to talk with prospective teachers about teacher research. Several individuals continue to talk quietly in pairs or small clusters for some time after.

What is unusual about this scene? Teachers are accustomed to being asked to attend meetings designed to carry out district agendas or mandates. It is far less common for teachers to organize themselves within a school system for purposes related to their own teaching and professional growth. The organization described here relied on both the resources of the school system and the voluntary contributions of teachers' time and work. This meeting of the Teacher Researcher Network was led by teachers and administrators who believe that teachers can and should direct their own professional organizations, including those that operate within the school system.

As an administrator who was a member of the Network, I asked my colleagues at the meeting for information to add to the data I had been collecting since the Network's beginning. I collected artifacts such as meeting notes, newsletters, and agendas; surveys and written responses from Network members; and taped dialogue from meetings and workshops. I took field notes in my research log and also wrote my own reflections.

In a large loose-leaf binder I arranged all but my field notes in chronological order and developed an annotated timeline of events for the life of the Network. As I collected data and wrote, I shared my drafts and questions with my Planning Group colleagues, enlisting their help in examination and analysis of the data while we participated as Network members.

Betsy Sanford explained her reasons for going to Network meetings, as she described its purposes:

> I go because I'm working on the task of protecting and supporting
> my professional identity as a teacher researcher. The Network
> helps make a place for the teacher research community. It reaches
> out and teaches people about teacher research.

Sanford's comments and the meeting described above reveal some important themes that recur in the story of the Network. It was conceived and has survived as an organization of teacher researchers who support each other professionally while seeking to educate and influence others in the school system who make policies that affect teachers and their classrooms. Its story is about the public, professional identities of teacher researchers. It is also a story characterized by and perhaps best understood in terms of its contradictions and paradoxes.

BOTH OLD AND NEW

What we don't have is a policy-making group.

The Network was both old and new. The participants at the first official meeting were already part of an informal network of teacher researchers who had been supporting one another since the first group of teacher researchers had organized in our district. Through the efforts of some, including teacher researchers who had moved into administrative roles, the school system had been quietly providing support for school-based groups of teacher researchers over nearly a decade and for an annual conference on teacher research the 3 preceding years. Teacher researchers in the district tended to know one another.

Other than at the conference, however, they did not regularly congregate; they did not comprise a discrete professional organization, and they did not collectively lobby for support. In the project proposal we had envisioned a structure to support this community of teacher researchers across the district. To begin anew, Planning Group members invited 25 colleagues in elementary, middle, and high schools to become members of a formalized teacher researcher network. All had provided leadership for teacher research in their schools or the district. We explained our vision of the Network in the invitation:

> The Network is intended to assist you in work that you are already doing and to provide a forum where the issues surrounding teachers' research can be discussed and information can be gathered and exchanged. The Network is also conceived as a place to discover new ways to disseminate information about teacher research to others.

At the first meeting of the Network, I welcomed participants and acknowledged the work we had been doing and the support we had given one another for years:

> What we don't have is a policy-making group—a broadly based group with the collective experience and expertise to consider the implications of teacher research for decision making in the school system—a group that could both support leadership for the work

that is already being done and find ways to help the system promote, support, and make effective use of that work.

We needed a collective voice.

Before exploring purposes and possibilities for the Network, participants wrote and talked in response to two questions: "What supports
teacher research? What stands in the way of teacher research?" Every one
of the 19 individuals identified time as essential to support and cited lack
of time as a major stumbling block. As one teacher researcher explained,

> Teacher research changes the way I look at my curriculum and my
> students. I need more time to think about what I am doing as a
> result. I need curriculum planning time with my grade level and
> interdisciplinary teams to incorporate the findings from my teacher
> research into my curriculum.

These were teachers who for years had been carving time out of their personal lives to compensate for what they could not find in their professional schedules.

Members' responses provided a vision for the Network. They saw the
value of teacher researcher findings to inform and shape school improvement
plans, curriculum design, program evaluation, and professional development.
They described the value of an "ongoing collection of data coming from students and teachers working together." And they cited the support of one
another: "Teacher research is about constant questioning about what is happening in the classroom and that means colleagues to sort things out with."

What stands in the way of this vision, they said, is "the idea that teachers
are the problem" and "the definition of a teacher as one who does things but
doesn't think." Although members cited the importance of system support for
teacher research, they did not ask the system to point the way. Leadership for
teacher research they saw as their professional responsibility. "What we're seeing is that people expect a lot of autonomy," Sanford would later observe.

During the meeting I wrote in my log that I felt good about this group of
experienced, committed people looking at direction for teacher research in our
district. I also wondered whether they could see the Network as supporting
their own work. "Or do they feel they've volunteered for another committee
to do work that they care about but that adds to their already overfull plates?"

A few months later I asked participants to write about their sense of the
Network's development so far and about their personal history in teacher
research. Everyone mentioned colleague support. They talked about the
connections they maintained with other teacher researchers even when they
were not conducting formal research.

Working with other teachers as they begin to see their teaching differently has helped me enormously. I have spent hours on the telephone and in long talks at conferences and in school parking lots. That person-to-person contact and concentration on our work in progress is at the core of any support system.

They stressed the need to be connected to other teacher researchers when they conduct research and to "participate in growing professional conversations that relate to theory and pedagogy." Like time, collaboration with colleagues was seen as critical to the process of conducting research.

I feel a great need for support in doing teacher research. . . . I have found I need people to talk to about learning. . . . Research is hard and at times threatening.

In my research log I reflected on the ways experienced teacher researchers created and directed this new, old network:

We spend a lot of time talking about the features of the system we inhabit, the locus of power, ways to educate . . . and to influence, . . . new ways to make teacher knowledge count. Experienced teacher researchers recognize the need to . . . move toward collective action and influence precisely because they value what research does in their professional lives, in their classrooms, their schools.

These are public school teachers who do not see their professionalism dependent on or directed by administrators or university professors. . . . Do Network participants see themselves as subversives or insiders? Some of both, I think. They recognize their efforts as largely grassroots, bottom-up, but they see the need for support from the top that provides validation for their work and access to resources they need.

REFLECTION AND ACTION

Maybe you don't create a formal network until you have an informal one already.

The kind of network experienced teacher researchers formed was one in which they were simultaneously reflective and activist, deliberately reflecting on the organization they were creating, but also conscious of the length of time required to accomplish objectives. As one member commented at the end of a meeting, "We're beginning to formalize this, but we still have a long way to go. . . . I think it will probably take the whole 3 years of the grant to build a structure that will stand alone."

In a meeting at the end of the first year, Network members gathered to consider the following questions "from both a research and a practical perspective": How does the Network provide leadership and direction for teacher research in our school district? How do we see ourselves providing leadership in the directions we have identified?

An animated discussion followed written reflection. Members talked about practical issues, including how to

- Provide access to resources and "good strong feedback" to teacher researchers on their work
- Promote the use of teachers' research through publication and dissemination
- Develop shared leadership for school-based groups of teacher researchers
- Provide experienced leaders for new school groups
- Create connections between teachers' research and school improvement initiatives
- Sustain teacher research in schools over time

The discussion also focused on the nature of the Network and its relationship to the school system. One member commented on the lack of "tradition for teachers to have . . . influence in a school" and the absence of "any kind of organizational structure or communication system within a school . . . that would utilize the expertise and knowledge of teachers." As the discussion continued, another member suggested, "Maybe you don't create a formal network until you have an informal one already."

Another member said that perhaps "teacher research challenges the leadership hierarchies that exist." Issues of position, power, and control were a backdrop to the stage on which the Network developed, but members approached such issues as data to be collected and examined in an attempt to reach understanding. I noted in my research log what seemed to be a pattern: "We talk about the issues and what needs to change, and then we move to what we need to do in the immediate future to move toward that change."

BALANCING SUPPORT AND ADVOCACY

It's important to realize the political consequences.

Could the Network create support for teacher researchers and provide a vehicle for influencing school system policies? The question persisted. As members talked about the future of the Network and implications for its structure, one member commented: "It's important to realize the political consequences. . . . I think the Network has two functions—one is to inform and the other is to support." While the balance was often uneasy, the Network attempted to do both.

Through its regular meetings, newsletter, and Web site the Network connected teacher researchers across schools, providing access to resources and informing a broad audience about activities and opportunities. Lone teacher researchers were invited to participate in neighboring school groups. Network members planned and organized the annual teacher researcher conference, providing teacher researchers a forum for presentation and discussion of their work and other teachers an introduction to teacher research and information about it.

The Network developed initiatives that would have been difficult if not impossible for individual teacher researchers to take on. They planned and provided the following opportunities:

- Workshops and seminars on topics such as starting and sustaining research groups, writing and publishing research, and connections between teacher research and school planning
- District-sponsored courses on teacher researcher group leadership and an introduction to teacher research
- Ongoing conversations about teacher research in the Network's newsletter, at its annual business meeting, and in seminars for district teachers and administrators

Many of the activities designed to support teacher researchers—the annual conference; seminars; workshops; presentations to and correspondences with administrators, parent and community groups, and teacher professional associations—also educated others about the effects and value of teacher research. Members published an article about the Network in the district's professional publication; made a presentation on teacher research to district school board members; and, with the local reading association, sponsored a breakfast for superintendents and school officials from several districts that featured their peers' endorsement of teacher research.

Through leadership roles in local, state, and national professional associations and presentations at their annual meetings and conferences, members linked the Network to the larger professional community and reminded the district of the significance of teacher research to educators across the nation. As one member observed, the Network "decided that the way you get support is by educating others."

BOTH VITAL AND TENUOUS

We don't have a vision of professionalism in teaching.

Members have considered and reconsidered some questions since the Network's beginning: What does a teacher researcher network look like, and how does it function? What are the roles of its members? What is its relationship to its individual members, to schools, to the school system?

The Network has lived a life at once vital and tenuous—its members have struggled to define, shape, and reshape it within the existing constraints of schedules, cultures, and politics. In my log I observed: "We may always be working out how the Network will develop; it's the nature of a network." Those of us who originally invited others to participate meant to create an initial framework that would allow participants to articulate purposes and organize to carry them out. We had in mind an organization led by teacher researchers themselves.

Keeping the Network teacher-directed was difficult because classroom teachers have the least amount of flexible time. Even 4 days of substitute leave for teachers to attend meetings the first year were too many for some members of the Network. After the first year, almost all meetings were held after contract hours. Teachers preferred to volunteer their personal time rather than be away from their students and out of their schools. Some participated consistently over the years while others came and went as their lives permitted.

Because teachers lacked time and resources, much of the organizing fell to those working in central offices. "If individuals out of the classroom take the lead in organizing, will the Network cease to be a teacher organization?" we asked ourselves. Sanford attributed "difficulty sustaining the Network" to the fact that "we don't have a vision of professionalism in teaching that would allow for [classroom teacher] members to have the resources to sustain it."

We had to think about roles and responsibilities based on such simple considerations as who had a telephone on her desk and a schedule not determined by class bells. For example, central office staff helped maintain the database for teacher researchers, coordinate Network meetings, and provide support and resources to the annual conference. Two teachers in resource roles in their schools, with schedules less confining than classroom teachers, served as co-chairs for the annual conference. A middle school classroom teacher served as editor of the newsletter with clerical support and resources from the central office. We struggled to build flexible structures and processes that would keep teachers involved in and shaping the direction of the Network.

It was not a question of teachers' ability to lead but one of conditions that made assuming leadership difficult. An entry in my log recalled a Planning Group discussion that recognized this quality of Network members: "These people didn't need leaders; they already are leaders."

A PART OF AND APART FROM

Participants . . . become political . . . even though that's not why they organized.

The Network had difficulty situating itself within or beside the school system. At the first meeting its new members talked about the benefits and risks of school system recognition and support for teacher research. Might institutionalization jeopardize the participation of teachers in research as voluntary? Might well-intentioned administrators require teachers to participate in programs with only superficial or even contrary connections to teacher research?

"I don't think that what comes out of teacher research is valued," one teacher researcher commented. Members understood that they were attempting to create a structure to provide support for something that they, not necessarily those in positions of power, saw the need to support. Sheila Clawson observed that the Network's role was "to continue to create that community . . . [that] establishes the credibility of teacher research in our school system," noting that no one teacher researcher can do that alone; "[we] need a community to do it."

As teacher researchers who regularly held up their work to the scrutiny of their colleagues, teachers had already taken on public roles. As Network members, they took on roles that became increasingly political, using their skills to understand the issues that affect teacher research and to influence policy in its favor. They saw this as part of their professional responsibility to themselves, their colleagues, their students, their schools, and their profession. Often they were behaving as professionals within a system that did not know how to deal with or support them. I reflected on the political role in my log:

While the work of teacher researchers is centered in schools, there needs to be institutional support for it.

Participants, once organized, become political to achieve their goals even though that's not why they organized. Implication: a network needs participants who know the system and have political experience.

INSIDERS AND OUTSIDERS

Insiders know, . . . outsiders come to know.

During the years of grant support, teacher research gained recognition within the school system; the Network contributed to that visibility. When the grant ended, the central office that had sponsored the grant continued to provide funds and support until a new administration presented an agenda that did not seem to signal room for teacher research. Network members—disappointed, but determined—took on the challenging role of convincing those in positions of power of its importance to teachers, students, and learning.

The most pressing business was to persuade school district policy makers to sustain some form of central office support for teacher research. When individual teacher researcher leaders were discouraged about the lack of district support, their collective participation in the Network kept alive the one remaining structure for advocacy.

Teacher research needed a designated place on the school system organizational chart, a home in a central office, and a telephone number in the directory. Network members used their connections to one another and to other teachers and administrators within the school system to capture the attention of system leaders. They carefully identified, articulated, and budgeted the essential elements needed. Their experience and learning as a network contributed to a clear sense of what was most critical to preserve and sustain, and they persisted in behaving as if their network were a necessary and essential part of the school system. Eventually, the Network found the listening ear of an assistant superintendent and connected itself to another central office. Still, its existence depends most heavily on the will and commitment of its members. It is their collective knowledge and action that will determine whether or not the Network continues and what shape it will take.

It seems appropriate, then, to close the still unfolding story of the Network by listening to Network members at the meeting described in the opening of this chapter speak about the recurring themes in the Network's history:

- The role of the Network is to support teacher researchers and to educate the broad educational community about the potential teacher research has for facilitating the growth and development of teachers—which in turn boosts student achievement. In order for teacher research to continue or flourish, it must be nurtured by the school system.
- The group plays an essential role in prolonging the life and existence of teacher research opportunities in [the school system]. . . . I think the Network's role must be to "beat the drums" until . . . heard . . . in hopes that people will get caught up in the "beat" and spread the word to others.
- The Network has long-range importance if it is a vehicle through which we can create a larger voice for teachers concerning decisions about the teaching and learning in their classrooms and schools. . . . The work that teacher researchers do is important, both . . . in terms of learning about teaching and learning, but also in terms of the climate of professional dialogue and exchange that teacher researchers within a school can create.
- The role of the Network, I feel, is to keep us "connected" and grounded. We have to know there are others who ask questions about their practice and that it's a way to promote teaching and change. . . . It helps us define our roles in ways that only insiders can know, but through the . . . research, outsiders can come to know.

As these teachers talk about why teacher research is important to them, they talk about their students' learning and about their teaching. They view their participation in the Network as both professional responsibility and sustenance, and they intend to have their collective voice heard. They are willing to contribute their time and talents to leading an organization that is powered by their own belief in the value of what they are doing for their students, their colleagues, and their school communities.

What Does Teacher Research in Schools Mean to the Educational Community?

In Part IV we present the implications of our research. Based on what we found out, how can our educational colleagues learn from and support teacher research in their schools? We open with five brief chapters of recommendations and practical advice, speaking directly to our readers, colleague to colleague. The recommendations are addressed to teachers, school-level administrators, central office administrators, teacher educators and professional developers, and parents and school communities. The final chapter is a discussion of our conclusions, arguing for teacher research in schools as a part of the school decision-making process.

CHAPTER 13

Recommendations for Teacher Colleagues

Betsy Sanford

In this chapter we address our teacher colleagues and discuss ways you might create and sustain a culture of teacher research in your classrooms, schools, and districts. Our recommendations are informed by our project research and our collective experience in teacher research over many years.

The recommendations are divided into four sections, starting with the most important ones as you establish a teacher research group, continuing with those that relate to the group's function within the school and community, and finishing with ones pertaining to districtwide support.

STARTING AND MAINTAINING A GROUP

As you consider starting a teacher research group in your school, knowing what issues to anticipate will help you set a course of action that will support your efforts. Our recommendations represent ways to be responsive to both the needs of teachers as well as the needs of the school as a whole.

- Start small.

    A teacher research group functions well with just a few people; larger groups present logistical difficulties that you may want to avoid initially.

- Be inclusive.

    Teacher research has no demographic group. Strength comes from a mix of grade levels, interests, and experience; each member both teaches and learns from the others.

- Consider how the group can provide support to its members.

    Colleagues in school-based teacher research groups help each other examine teaching practices, question unexamined assumptions, and explore tentative connections or contradictions. As you plan how the group will function, look for ways to promote exchanges that will foster such support.

- Expect that members will vary in their understanding and level of commitment to the research process.

  Disparities in research experience and level of commitment are common in a teacher research group, and the group will have to accommodate those disparities. Regardless of their differences, however, all participants need the support of colleagues, and each will contribute to the group's strength.

- Balance the group's goal to be inclusive with its need for commitment from members.

  Occasionally colleagues join the research group even though they are unable to commit to it fully. This is rarely satisfactory, since it affects the support that other members receive. In such a case, it's important to consider the group's needs and to recommend postponing teacher research until circumstances are more favorable.

- Discuss, promote, and safeguard ethical research practices.

  From the outset, the group should establish ethical research guidelines. These include maintaining student privacy, treating research participants fairly and with respect, obtaining parent permission before using student work samples, acknowledging both contradictory and confirming data in the study, and respecting district policies that may have an impact on research decisions. If you have concerns about the ethics of your own research or those of a colleague, voice them and seek dialogue and resources.

- Be prepared for the tensions of competing, entrenched views about teaching.

  Teacher researchers can be genuinely committed to improved understanding and yet hold some beliefs intractably. Group members must challenge respectfully the views of colleagues that seem problematic or dissonant. While such discussions may not seem immediately fruitful, they can prompt reevaluation, rethinking, and reseeing.

- Give it time!

  Teacher research operates with a ripple effect in schools, acting first upon group members and only later on school policies and long-range planning. The impact of a group and the research studies it generates may take several years to be felt.

REACHING OUT AND GARNERING SUPPORT

The more others know about a research group's efforts, the more quickly they will recognize the value to the school of such a group. There are several avenues for seeking support for the group.

- Promote collegial exchange in your school.

  A school-based teacher research group engages in a conversation about teaching that is sustained, significant, and multivoiced. Teacher researchers can extend the conversation by sharing their research interests, findings, and implications with colleagues. They can also have an impact through serving on committees responsible for guiding school improvement efforts. Over time the dialogue prompted by sharing research can be a catalyst for schoolwide change.

- Distribute teacher research articles to colleagues, administrators, and parents.

  When teacher researchers write final reports of their research, they gain deeper understanding of their teaching and their students' learning. Don't let those articles sit on the shelf! Distribute them. Better yet, encourage your teacher researcher colleagues to prepare summaries of their articles for colleagues, administrators, and parents who may become valuable supporters of your school's research efforts.

- Encourage parents to become better informed about teacher research.

  The parent community is often an untapped source of support for teacher research. Make parents aware of the research initiative at your school and how teacher research can affect student achievement.

- Encourage parent and community groups to support a teacher research initiative.

  Community groups such as PTAs are excellent places to promote awareness of teacher research and its connections to improved student achievement. Encourage parents who support teacher research to communicate that support to the school board, central office personnel, and the community at large.

WHOSE SCHOOL IS IT, ANYWAY?

Perhaps because the effects of teacher research start quietly and take time to gain momentum, it is easy for school staffs to ignore the importance of research efforts. There are several strategies that will help keep your group from being marginalized both in the school's organizational plan and in its culture.

- Expect to be able to teach and do research.

  Teacher researchers who feel tension between their regular teaching responsibilities and their research responsibilities should keep two ideas in mind. First, remember that good teacher research is good teaching because its goal is understanding. Second, make your research a priority. If you make the choice to teach and do research, find ways to accomplish what you set out to do in your research, knowing that improved student achievement is your real objective.

- Promote school policies that provide teachers with flexibility.

  The highly constrained schedules of most teachers present research challenges. Teacher researchers conduct studies and change their instructional methods in response to what they learn. A school culture that allows for the revision of teaching plans and methods supports this kind of work. If teacher researchers are to support each other, they also need to be able to observe in each other's classrooms and meet with individual students or small groups. Scheduling flexibility on even a small scale can assist the work of teacher researchers.

- Consider a link between teacher research and evaluation.

  Some districts use teacher research as an evaluation component. Those districts recognize that conducting teacher research signifies a teacher's commitment to examine teaching and learning. Tying teacher research to evaluation involves complex issues. Districts seeking to link teacher research and evaluation should keep in mind the principles of teacher research, that it is intentional, systematic, public, voluntary, ethical, and contextual.

- Expect that your work can inform your school's instructional program and school improvement plan.

  Teacher researchers revise aspects of their teaching based on their research findings, although they often hesitate to recommend schoolwide revisions. However, making public their findings can lead to improving the instructional program in the entire school, and they should plan to share their expertise.

APPROPRIATING RESOURCES

Teacher research is not an expensive program to institute or maintain, but there are important resources that can lend viability to a research initiative.

- Seek to include teacher research in your school's and district's professional development program.

  Teacher researchers can work to assure that teacher research is included as an option for professional development. A school's or district's professional development program should also capitalize on the work of teacher researchers. Their work should be acknowledged and used, through research presentations and the dissemination of their written studies.

- Seek district or university sponsorship of teacher research.

  Courses that guide teachers as they learn about and engage in teacher research support both new and experienced teacher researchers. In our area, several course options have been available over the past few years:

  * a graduate-level seminar in teacher research
  * masters' programs with teacher research components
  * a 5-week introductory course on teacher research
  * a course to help teachers develop strategies for reflective practice
  * a course to help teacher researchers prepare to lead a teacher research group
  * a program to pair experienced teacher researcher group leaders with teacher researchers learning to lead

- Seek possible funding and support from professional development and curriculum development offices.

  The modest costs involved in teacher research make it attractive, but lack of awareness by those who control funding can keep it from being included in the budget. Seek funding from your district's professional development budget; consider focusing your research on curriculum development in general and seek curriculum development funds; investigate grants as possible funding sources. While funding sometimes comes with additional obligations, it also gives the group visibility and legitimacy in the eyes of some observers.

- Consider how district resources might be used to develop and support the teacher research community.

  Whether your district is large or small, it has resources you can use to circulate teacher research opportunities, announce conferences, highlight teacher research groups, publicize teacher researcher events, and disseminate research studies. Evaluate your district's existing resources and plan ways a teacher research community might use them.

We know that efforts to start and sustain teacher research groups come with challenges as well as exhilaration. We hope the advice included here will provide you with guidance in your efforts. We hope, too, that knowing some of the challenges you can expect will enable you to prepare for them. The prospect of increased understanding of teaching and learning, deepened collegial respect, and greater professional satisfaction will make your efforts worthwhile.

CHAPTER 14

Recommendations for School-Level Administrators

Mary Ann Nocerino

Principal support for teacher research, beyond simple approval, was critical in our research project schools. The following recommendations are for principals and other school-level administrators as you think about what may be appropriate for you and your school. Suggestions for launching a group of teacher researchers are followed by suggestions for sustaining a group and for using the work of teacher researchers to benefit the school.

LAUNCHING A GROUP

Careful consideration about ways to support teacher researchers at the beginning of their work can help ensure success for their efforts.

- Obtain the expertise of an experienced teacher researcher when starting a research group.

  It is essential that an inexperienced teacher researcher group have support in learning research skills such as identifying research questions, collecting and analyzing data, determining results, and drawing implications for teaching and learning. An experienced teacher researcher or teacher researcher leader can reside in your school, another school, the central office, or a university. Professional organizations such as local chapters of the International Reading Association or the National Writing Project are also good places to contact for information and recommendations.

- Encourage participation in a teacher researcher group, but keep it voluntary.

  Teacher research is a commitment to looking closely at student learning and at one's teaching. It requires time for teachers to learn and practice research procedures. Teacher research is not for everyone, nor is it always appropriate at a given time in one's life. Other demands on a teacher, both personal and professional, may compete for time and energy.

- Send pizza!

  Recognize the commitment teachers are making as they begin a group by providing some tangible symbols. One principal provided pizza for participants at the first meeting; another brought a rose for each member of the group.

- Provide practical support for teacher researchers and the teacher researcher leader.

  Protect their time and schedule. All three schools set up a schedule for teacher research meetings early in the year so they were included on the master calendar. Competing demands in schools are rampant and having a slot on the school's master calendar helps to protect the time for teacher researchers to meet.

- Provide space and substitute teachers.

  Provide space for meetings in the building where interruptions will be limited as much as possible. Teacher researchers also find it helpful occasionally to meet away from the school to provide for concentrated periods of time to discuss their research and develop data collection strategies. Business partners are a source for meeting space, as well as county government facilities, or school district meeting spaces.

  Occasional extended meetings are needed during the day when teachers are fresh, not at the end of a workday, and substitute time is one way to provide that time for teacher researchers. Grant, PTA, and staff development funding, as well as principal discretionary monies are some ways to patch together substitute time funding.

SUSTAINING A GROUP AND BENEFITING A SCHOOL

The following are suggestions for sustaining a group of teacher researchers in your school and benefiting from the work, skills, and talents of teacher researchers.

- Familiarize yourself with teachers' research.

  You need to know what teachers are learning through their research. The principals in the project schools read the research drafts of the teacher researchers. Marvin Spratley, the high school principal, came to the meeting of the research group after receiving a copy of the research drafts, stating that he stayed up late the previous night reading the articles, and then proceeded to discuss the findings. Attending research meetings toward the end of the research process and informal conversations with teacher researchers are other ways to familiarize yourself with teachers' research.

- Use teachers' research to change school policy.

    One of the best ways to support teacher research is to use it to inform decisions when developing or changing school policy. For example, when principal June Monterio read Leslie Asip's research on inclusion of learning disabled students in general education classrooms at the middle school level, she recognized implications for the kind of support and scheduling learning disabled students needed at her school.

- Use teachers' research when working with parents.

    Teachers' research can be a resource for your work with parents. For example, principal Marvin Spratley remembered social studies teacher Bill Plitt's research on goal setting when he was working with parents whose children would soon enter the school as ninth graders. The parents were concerned about their children's adjustment to high school and the self-discipline needed to study and succeed. Plitt's research examined how goal setting was an important strategy that students used to help them accomplish their work. Making such connections requires knowledge about the research, making it important that you are familiar with the teachers' findings.

- Assist teacher researchers in disseminating their research findings.

    There are many ways administrators support teacher researchers in sharing the research findings. Principals provide clerical support and materials for compiling teachers' research articles in school publications. Publication parties including refreshments for the staff highlight the research in a festive way. Some principals write an introduction to the school publication that helps to endorse the work of teacher researchers. Principals in the project schools provided time for teachers to share their research with staff at team and faculty meetings in informal roundtable discussion groups where staff members chose the research topics about which they wanted to learn.

- Work closely with the teacher researcher leader to discuss ways to support the research group.

    Principals and teacher researcher leaders in the project invented ways to support teacher research appropriate to their schools.

Sheila Clawson helped the principal draft a letter to send to teachers during the summer inviting them to participate in the teacher research group in the fall. Using the principal's conference room for meetings and featuring research findings at faculty meetings are ideas that evolved when principals and teacher researcher leaders thought together about how to support the research group.

- Tap into teacher researcher skills when conducting schoolwide needs assessments and developing long range plans for the school.

  More and more schools are developing school plans that provide direction for the school and a means of accountability to the school division and the community. Good planning is based on data—to determine goals and to monitor progress in meeting those goals. Teacher researchers have skills in data collection and analysis. For example, the high school in the project examined block scheduling through the use of a survey that used both qualitative and quantitative research strategies that the teacher researcher leader provided.

- Include teacher researchers on school planning teams or other committees where the research can be disseminated and used to make school decisions.

  Including teacher researchers on planning committees facilitates the sharing and use of the knowledge gained from research for school decision making in the natural course of conducting school business. Research findings can inform instructional strategies as well as raise issues for the school. For example, findings of a group of middle school teacher researchers pointed to the common need for reading instruction in the content areas. Emerging from the research was a yearlong staff development program in teaching reading across the content areas.

- Conduct research on your own practice.

  One way to understand the effects of practitioner research is to conduct research on your own practice as a principal. In some school districts small groups of administrators have formed principal research groups. Participating in a principal research group has potential for improving your own practice as well as providing you with insight into ways that you can support teachers who do so.

CHAPTER 15

Recommendations for Central Office Administrators

Courtney Rogers

Over the course of our project we dreamed about an "Office of Teacher Research." We envisioned the staffing and functions of such an office, but we know of no school district that has one. Colleagues in other districts support teacher research from offices responsible for staff development, curriculum and instruction, or teacher evaluation. In a small district in our state a high school teacher researcher went to an assistant superintendent and convinced her to provide funding and support for a project. In a neighboring district the superintendent endorsed teacher research as one option for teacher evaluation. Most administrators we know who support teacher research do so in the context of their roles and responsibilities and the shifting priorities and politics of their districts.

In my central office position I was fortunate to work with a colleague, Mary Ann Nocerino, who shared my commitment to teacher research. We sought institutional recognition of the connections we saw between teacher research and the mission of our office, which was to support schools in improving student achievement. But it was our collaborative relationships with teacher colleagues that were critical to providing support for teacher research in our district.

What follows are five broad categories, each with two or three recommendations for central office administrators. In some cases suggested practices are illustrated with examples from our experience. Since some of the recommendations may challenge existing assumptions, roles, and structures in your district, you will need to decide what is most important and what is feasible to accomplish.

BUILDING A KNOWLEDGE BASE ABOUT TEACHER RESEARCH

While it is useful to read the literature on teacher research, particularly that which is authored by teacher researchers, an understanding of classroom research based on experience is invaluable.

- Educate yourself about teacher research.

    Administrators can learn by conducting inquiry on aspects of their own practice. For example, an administrator who works with new teachers might ask, "How do I support beginning teachers' efforts to balance instructional planning with classroom management?" Another effective way to educate yourself is to visit and observe teacher researcher groups. An important resource is the nearest National Writing Project site; contact them and inquire about teacher research.

- Share what you are learning with your colleagues.

    Identify one or more colleagues who are interested in working with you to initiate or support teacher research in your district. Also identify experienced teacher researchers in your own or nearby districts and invite them to work with you and your colleagues. Remember (and remind your colleagues) that no matter how excited you become about the potential of teacher research to improve student learning and schools, it needs to be voluntary.

PROVIDING SUPPORT FOR TEACHER RESEARCH

Once teacher research has gained a foothold in your district, you will need to look for ways to help it grow and flourish. The following suggestions are just a few ways that support can be provided.

- Invite teachers to organize a districtwide network of teacher researchers and provide resources to support them.

    Central office administrators can work collaboratively with teacher researcher leaders. In our district, members of the Teacher Researcher Network set priorities and decided on both short-range and long-range plans for support of teacher research. From our office came resources, some grant funding, and logistical support for the Network and its activities, such as the annual conference.

- Use experienced teacher researcher leaders to provide training and support for teachers who want to learn to conduct classroom research.

    As interest in school-based teacher research groups grows, help by coordinating resources and providing guidance. Support for a new school group is time and labor intensive. It can involve helping to organize and facilitate regular meetings for the first year or two. As more schools become interested and more teachers gain experience in research, support can be customized to the existing experience, expertise, and leadership in each school.

- Offer courses related to teacher research through your district's staff development office.

  Design and promote courses that will support the development of teachers as researchers and offer participants teacher recertification points or graduate credit. Courses offered in our district included Introduction to Teacher Research, Developing Strategies for Reflective Practice, and Learning to Lead a Teacher Researcher Group in a School Setting.

SUPPORTING THE DISSEMINATION OF TEACHER RESEARCH

Once teachers have conducted research, your job will include encouraging them to participate in the broader professional discourse.

- Help teacher researchers write and publish their research.

  Read and respond to individual drafts of research studies by teacher researchers as they prepare the in-house publications of their reports. You can also make teacher researchers aware of publication opportunities beyond their school and district and provide support as those teachers seek publication in professional journals.

- Provide local forums for teacher researchers to share their research.

  You can help individual school research groups plan small, informal inservice programs for sharing their research with school colleagues and neighboring schools. You can also initiate a collaboration among teachers, administrators, and local professional organizations to provide a larger scale forum, perhaps an annual teacher researcher conference.

- Support teachers' presentation of their research at regional and national meetings of professional organizations.

  The culture of most school districts makes it easy for teachers to avoid venturing beyond their classrooms or schools to share their expertise and contribute to the professional dialogue. Teachers' reluctance to go public is understandable: There are relatively few models for teacher experts, lesson plans for substitutes take time (making leaving one's classroom difficult), and time away from the classroom may mean lower student productivity.

Central office funds in many school districts are more likely to support the travel and conference-related expenses of administrators than of classroom teachers. Funding substitutes for their classes, paying a portion of conference and travel fees, and providing stipends for work beyond contract hours to prepare presentations of their research are three ways to help overcome this inequity.

EDUCATING OTHERS ABOUT TEACHER RESEARCH

- Work collaboratively with teacher and administrator colleagues to inform other administrators, teachers, and parents about teacher research.

  Encourage teacher researchers to inform their principals about their teacher research activities. Work with teacher researcher colleagues to design district-sponsored workshops informing school administrators and teachers about the effects of teacher research in schools. Knowledgeable school-based and district administrators can share their experiences with other administrators at local and national seminars and meetings. Plan joint presentations to parent and community groups. With teacher researcher colleagues, copresent findings at professional conferences about the effects of teacher research on teacher practice, student learning, and school reform.

- Talk to policy makers about teacher research.

  Make presentations to school board members and school officials intended to help them see distinctions between teacher research and other forms of staff development, the cost effectiveness of providing time for teachers to work in teacher research groups, and the value of leadership roles for teachers in their schools and district. Some education efforts will be more successful than others, some audiences more receptive than others. However, education is an ongoing process as school board members and school officials come and go.

TEACHER RESEARCHERS AS LEADERS

Intentionally or unintentionally, some districts pay lip service to teacher leadership without creating opportunities for teachers to serve in leadership roles. Our research indicates that teacher researchers know a great deal about how they learn that can inform decisions about resources and plans in a district. In addition, teachers' research can inform their schools' efforts to improve student achievement as well as curriculum development at the school and district levels.

- Include teacher researcher leaders in designing district support for teacher research.

  In establishing the Teacher Research Network, our central office helped create a structure that supported the development of teacher research leadership in the district. Such an organization can lobby for district support of teacher research and can serve as a source for advice on shaping future support. Such a collaborative effort is especially valuable because it gives a central and powerful voice to teacher researchers.

- Invite teacher researchers to share ways in which their research has informed school planning and evaluation.

  In workshops for school planning teams, invite teacher researcher participants to describe how their research has contributed to identifying, shaping, or monitoring student achievement objectives in their schools.

- Invite teacher researchers to present their research on teaching content.

  Curriculum specialists can look for ways to include teacher researchers in district inservices, inviting them to share what they have learned from conducting research. Teacher researchers can also make valuable contributions by serving on committees whose responsibilities include reviewing, writing and revising curriculum.

QUESTIONS RAISED BY OUR RECOMMENDATIONS

Our research indicates that the role of the central office administrator needs to shift as teachers assume leadership roles in their schools and district and take on increased responsibility for their own professional development. It also raises many questions: How can responsibilities be shared with equal status and with respect to the ease and efficiency of accomplishing tasks? How can the research process and an understanding of data-driven decision making be used by both schools and central office staff? How can the findings of teacher research become a part of central office knowledge and curriculum planning? We ask your help in answering these questions.

CHAPTER 16

Recommendations for Teacher Educators and Professional Developers

Marion S. MacLean

The most important recommendation coming from our findings for teachers' professional development concerns the shift teacher research requires in the relationship between teachers and teacher educators. Teacher researchers' professional growth is deeply connected to their research through self-direction and choice. Their individual choices about participation, their decisions about research focus, their selections of kinds of data to analyze, their focus on their own classrooms, and their determination of their own questions about their students' learning all weigh heavily in establishing the potential for growth. This degree of teacher choice and autonomy is often missing in traditional forms of teacher education and staff development that focus on generic problems (like classroom management) addressed by implementing a particular program across a school or a district.

CHANGING ROLES

When teacher educators and professional developers work with teacher researchers, they play a different kind of role. As both a teacher educator and a classroom teacher researcher, I have by necessity examined both roles in my own career as well as in our project research. I hope that the following discoveries are useful to you:

- Teacher research requires the support, opportunities, perspectives, and knowledge that university instructors and staff developers can offer, including experience with different research methodologies, both qualitative and quantitative.
- Working with those who have knowledge of the field of educational research can help teacher researchers see how their own work

can contribute to knowledge in that field and can validate the
work in their own eyes.

- Teacher educators can work to understand the nature of teacher
  research, teacher research processes and strategies, the issues that
  complicate teacher research, and the experience of conducting
  research on one's own practice as they provide guidance to teacher
  researchers.
- Teacher educators can provide resources to support teacher
  researchers. For example, university colleagues may be able to
  bring teachers from different schools together to work on their
  research in courses taught at the university.
- School system professional developers can create time (released
  time, substitute leave, or after-school meeting time) for teacher
  researchers in a district or building to meet.
- School system administrators can select and promote teacher
  research as one of the options a school system might offer for
  teachers' professional development or evaluation.
- Conducting your own teacher research as you work with a group of
  teacher researchers can support both the process and the outcome
  of the research. This can add to the general understanding of how
  teacher researchers learn and to your own understanding of your
  teaching.
- University and school district teacher educators can help others
  make use of the knowledge that teachers create as part of their
  research. This is a new role for many teacher educators used to seeing their job as bringing to teachers what others know. It might
  help to think through the following questions as you explore this
  role:
  * How can school-based teacher research be disseminated across
    a district?
  * Which teacher research reports contribute to your goals, plans,
    and efforts? How can you make use of them in programs you
    are planning?
  * How can teacher researchers from different schools arrange to
    meet with each other to share their work?
  * When your district sets a particular goal systemwide, how can
    teacher researchers fit their questions into the broad perspective
    of that goal? How can their findings be disseminated to others
    interested in the goal?
  * What professional meetings and conferences would be of bene-
    fit to teacher researchers? How could their travel be financed?
  * What grants are available that could accept proposals for teach-

ers' research? How could you assist teacher researchers in applying?

* What publications would be interested in teacher researchers' articles? How could you support teacher researchers in seeking professional publication of their work?

GRADUATE PROGRAMS AND COURSES

In general, if you are a university teacher of teachers, you have the opportunity to contribute a great deal toward the professionalism of teaching through teacher research. In our own community a local university has established a master's degree program based on school teams that conduct teacher research. Sites of the National Writing Project support teacher professionalism and often have teacher research groups as part of their programs. Your local school district may have some teacher research groups in their schools who would welcome university support or credit.

These opportunities take a variety of forms, from school system credit to graduate-level university courses. A wide range of offerings allows teachers to choose those that best meet their needs. Whether teachers are involved in reflective practices or in full-fledged research projects, recognition in the form of credit, compensatory time, points toward recertification, and other tangible forms of recognition legitimize the substantial work that these teachers do. Universities and professional development offices offer recognition not only in the eyes of teachers, but also in the eyes of school administrators, school systems, and universities.

As colleagues in the effort to improve the quality of teaching in the schools, teacher researchers, teacher educators, and professional developers have much to offer each other. Schools are served best by educators and researchers who work deliberately to respect and incorporate the knowledge from their different perspectives about the teaching and learning of their students.

CHAPTER 17

Recommendations for
Parents and School Communities

Marian M. Mohr

Teacher researchers often communicate with the parents of their students by letter because the form allows them to discuss their research with carefully chosen words, yet to speak informally. For similar reasons these recommendations are written as a letter, personal yet based on the implications of our research. This letter is meant to aid in your understanding of what teacher research means and how it can benefit your child's education.

*   *   *

Dear Parents,

First-grade teacher Betsy Sanford writes a newsletter to her students' parents called "The Math Corner." In it she describes her past research with first graders on learning mathematics, and she lists some things she has learned that might be useful to parents in their efforts to help their children learn mathematics. Her research is no secret; she invites the parents to a workshop on multiplication and division. Her tone is direct, personal, and friendly.

Teacher researchers, like Sanford, often write to parents in a letter at the beginning of the year telling them about their classroom research. A slip asking for permission to quote your child may be enclosed, or a request to use some written work as part of a professional presentation or an article the teacher is preparing. You may be asked to help in the research by answering some questions or working with your child in some special way.

How should you react to the news that your child's teacher is also a researcher? In this letter I will offer you some ideas based on my experience as a teacher, parent, and researcher.

First of all, I think your child is lucky to have a teacher researcher. Teacher researchers are studying how their teaching and their students' learning work together. They examine their students' work—their papers, projects, and homework—as well as what they say about their learning.

They keep notes about the lessons and analyze and evaluate them. They may audio- or videotape a class so that they have a record of what happened to analyze later. Sometimes the students help out by keeping track of their learning, perhaps on a poster on the wall or in a computer database.

This may not sound like what you may ordinarily think of as research, that is, statistical or experimental studies with controlled variables. Such research can tell us about large numbers of people or very limited groups of people who are very similar, especially when we want to give them all a dose of the same thing. But students are not the same, and they do not all learn in the same way. Teachers study the results of statistical studies, but more importantly, they need to know the hows and whys. Why are the test scores what they are? How can I help my students learn mathematics? What happens when I use this teaching method? Teacher researchers ask questions that are important to them in their own classrooms and, with their students' help, systematically seek answers.

Sometimes teachers include parents in their research. Julie Lindquist (1999), a middle school teacher, wrote about her research in her article "Independent Reading: Just Do It!" Lindquist set up an independent reading program with her students to investigate ways to encourage them to read more. They chose the books they wanted to read, and their parents kept a record of their reading with their children, even giving them a grade at the end of the quarter. Of her 135 students, only 3 sets of parents did not participate!

Lindquist kept track of the parents' responses as well as the students'. She changed her program a little bit each quarter in response to the data she received. One quarter she offered an extra-credit project where students and their parents read together. Students said that being able to discuss the book with a parent helped them see things they might have missed. Parents were impressed by what their children knew about literature. In some cases the students knew English better than their parents but benefited from their parents' life experience in interpreting what they read. At the same time they helped their parents learn English.

I am describing a teacher who sees herself as a learner along with her students. Teacher researchers ask questions that they don't know the answers to as well as those they do. Something else you might notice in a teacher researcher's classroom is that they watch and observe classroom events before responding to them, and they take seriously what their students tell them about their learning.

A wonderful side effect for your son or daughter in a teacher researcher's classroom is getting to see an adult learner at work, seeing how their teacher solves problems, discusses dilemmas, and tries different ways to understand things. To a teacher researcher, a student's errors in a math assignment are interesting! He wants to find out why the errors appeared and what might help the student learn. A teacher researcher treats learning problems as research questions.

Teacher research is very useful in the classroom, but it is also a way to resolve and understand things in the school as a whole, especially if the school has a group of teachers conducting research. They can investigate questions important to the school and help evaluate school programs, such as computer learning, or new curriculum being introduced, such as a new literature program. They can help the school make decisions about its programs based on data and research, not just on opinion or resistance to change.

If you want to volunteer at your child's school, consider participating in classroom research. You might be able to help one of the teacher researchers on her study, perhaps doing an observation or making a videotape to analyze later. Perhaps you have a question of your own and would like to join the school research group.

My children never had the perfect teachers I wanted for them as a parent, but I knew, as a teacher, that they needed to know from me that they were good learners and that learning was important. I knew also how hard it was to do a good job of teaching. My own failures were always staring me in the face whenever I felt ready to criticize my children's teachers.

When I began to view my teaching through the lens of research, I saw possibilities for understanding and improving my teaching, and when I had the opportunity to watch other teacher researchers at work, I saw that they had found a way to keep on learning about teaching and to make their learning useful to their students.

So, if you get a letter from one of your children's teachers talking about his or her research project, it should be an interesting year. If you learn more about teacher research and think it is a good thing, talk to your Parent Teacher Association about it, and perhaps invite some of the teacher researchers to report on what they are finding out. Your Parent Teacher Association might let the school board know that teacher research is professional development for teachers that helps students learn.

Cathy Fleischer (1998), a university teacher researcher, writes about several different teacher researchers who made the effort to explain the findings of their research to their parent communities and school boards. They wanted to combine their research with action in their local communities. As Betsy Sanford does in "The Math Corner," these teacher researchers skillfully combined teaching and researching, becoming better teachers of your children and your professional allies in their education.

Sincerely yours,
A Teacher Researcher and Parent

REFERENCES

Fleischer, C. (1998). Advocating for change: A new education for new teachers. *English Education, 30,* 78–100.

Lindquist, J. (1999). Independent reading: Just do it! In M. S. MacLean & M. M. Mohr, *Teacher-researchers at work* (pp. 180–194). Berkeley, CA: National Writing Project.

CHAPTER 18

How Teacher Research Can Affect Decision Making in the Educational Community

It is teachers who, in the end, will change the world of school by understanding it.

—Lawrence Stenhouse (1985)

Throughout the teacher research in schools project we each pursued individual research interests. The findings and interpretations of our studies fill Parts II and III. But we also augmented our individual research with data collected in response to the general questions that, as a group, we had raised originally, questions that formed the basis for the project. Often the individual studies and the general questions overlapped.

As the data widened, our understanding deepened. We think that readers planning to support teacher research groups in their schools need a panoramic view as well as a narrowly focused one. The purpose of this chapter is to present our common findings, ones that the group as a whole agreed upon based on the data as a whole.

We will first list the findings as answers to our central questions—an overview that includes ideas previously introduced in individual studies as well as new ones. After the overview, we will present three themes which grew in importance in our thinking as our analysis progressed. Each will be discussed along with its implications. Taken together, they offer evidence and suggestions for supporting teacher research in schools.

SUMMARY OF COMMON FINDINGS

What happened when teachers conducted research as members of school groups?

- They developed research questions from the issues and events of their own classrooms in relation to their students' learning.

- Their questions were frequently related to school wide issues and had relevance to their school communities.
- From the daily events of their classrooms, they collected and interpreted data and developed findings.
- They developed research skills to assess and monitor student achievement.
- They saw teaching implications in their findings and changed their teaching as a result.
- They wrote to document and understand their research and to disseminate their findings.
- They gave presentations to colleagues about their work.
- They saw implications from their research findings for their schools and school district.

How do teaching and learning look in the classrooms of teacher researchers?

- Teacher researchers taught in ways that engaged their students, addressed their individual needs, and modeled the behavior of a learner.
- They examined their students' learning and their own teaching to inform their instructional decision making.
- They and their students acquired the expectation that they would all contribute their knowledge about learning to the classroom curriculum.
- They and their students developed a repertoire of learning strategies to use as they took on new learning tasks.
- They achieved a managed distance from their practice that enabled them to analyze, evaluate, and revise their teaching.
- They viewed researching as a way of learning, errors as useful data, and teaching as a process of conducting research.

What happened when teacher researcher leaders had reassigned time to provide leadership for school groups?

- Leaders developed a style different from traditional notions of leadership; they led with and beside their colleagues.
- They developed reciprocal, collegial relationships with their administrators.
- They provided training in research methodology for teacher researchers and support for their research.
- They helped teacher researchers disseminate their findings among their colleagues.

- They promoted the use of the group's findings in school decision making.
- They took on increased leadership roles in their schools.
- They provided leadership for teacher research in their district and in the greater educational community.

What were the effects of teacher researcher groups on their schools and their district?

- Teacher researchers created learning communities in their schools.
- They directed their professional growth in ways that addressed the needs of their students and school community.
- They developed a perspective on the school as a whole and the need for collective action to improve teaching and learning in the school.
- They developed skills in data collection, analysis, and collaborative work with colleagues on schoolwide issues.
- Their research contributed to assessment of existing school programs and generated new programs.
- Teacher researcher communities in different schools collaborated with each other to exchange information and support professional development.
- The Teacher Researcher Network designed and implemented programs to support teacher research districtwide.
- The Teacher Researcher Network educated policy makers about teacher research and advocated for district support of teacher research.
- Some teacher researchers moved beyond their schools and district to publish in national journals and give presentations on their research at state and national conferences.

How did administrators respond to teacher research groups in their schools?

- Administrators supported teacher research by endorsing the use of substitute leave time for teacher researchers to work together, reading and acknowledging the teacher research studies, and promoting the work of teacher researchers among faculty and in school planning.
- They saw teacher research as centered on student learning and promoted the use of teacher researcher knowledge to inform teaching and learning in classrooms.
- They valued the leadership of the teacher researcher leaders and formed collegial relationships with them.

- They recognized the potential for teachers' research to inform school decision making about curriculum and programs.
- They demonstrated the value they placed on teacher research by contributing to efforts to educate others in the school system about teacher research.

THEMES FROM THE FINDINGS

As we talked through our findings, we saw that a lot of what had happened was a result of the reassigned time available to the teacher researcher leaders, MacLean, Clawson, and Sanford; the substitute leave time for the teacher researchers in the schools; the "in-kind" time given to the central office administrators, Nocerino and Rogers; and the research time available to the school liaison, Mohr. We had funding to buy time and the expectation that the time would be used for research. We had time to try things we had often thought about, such as building a teacher research network, and time to gather information about educational questions beyond the classroom, such as how teacher research affects a school.

The expectation that time would be used for teacher research even caused a shift in our thinking about how time already available was used. We saw that time researching is also time teaching. Time on school committees could also be time in a teacher researcher group. Time developing a school's goals and objectives could also be time spent disseminating the findings of teacher research. For a while, at least, teacher research was on an equal footing with existing committees and expected responsibilities.

Supported by time and expectations, teachers conducted research and saw it as contributing to their students' learning. They also began to see it as helpful to their teaching colleagues and to their schools' planning and evaluating. They adopted a view of themselves as professionals outside the classroom as well as inside. Along with this professionalism came a growing understanding of the connections between their individual research and school policies and professional development programs.

School policies and professional development programs, while they may be conducted with some teacher "input," are usually developed and decided upon by people in the school district who are not in the classroom. Teachers are expected to comply with their decisions. They are not considered decision makers or sources of knowledge and information that would be of use in the process. Even in situations where teachers' involvement may be valued, it is deemed impractical—they don't have the time.

The three general themes just described briefly—the use of teachers' time, teachers as professionals, and the connections between teacher research and school plans and programs—are elaborated in the discussion that follows. Emerging from each discussion are some implications for schools and school districts. We will be writing about these ideas separately, but they are cumulative and interdependent.

TIME FOR TEACHER RESEARCH IN SCHOOLS: DISCUSSION

Time dedicated to self-directed professional development is a rarity. The time provided by the grant consistently played a critical role in the success of the project. It was important not only to teachers conducting research, but also to the teacher researcher leaders as they supported the research efforts in their schools. Beyond the schools, time was also critical in creating and sustaining the Network and in project planning and decision making.

Time to Conduct Research

The one-year length of a research project, while arbitrary, had the advantage of synchronizing the research process with the school calendar. With experimentation and trial we learned that 2–3-hour meetings resulted in deeper discussions than 1 hour. An important element of timing the meetings was assisting the teachers in retaining, or regaining, their concentration on their research. Also, a meeting had to offer time for every teacher researcher, including the leader, to write and talk about his or her own research as well as to respond to others.

Although some teachers stayed in research groups for only one year, during the second and third years we looked at time from the point of view of teacher researchers who remained in the group. They did not need the same experience as first-year teacher researchers, and what they needed differed from teacher to teacher. Some of them wanted a year away from research, but wished to continue attending the group meetings, serving as teacher research mentors to the new researchers and sharing the responsibilities of leading the group. Others wanted to extend their first year's research in a different direction, and still others had a new question to investigate. Some wanted to spend less time on writing; some wanted to spend more.

Teacher Researcher Leaders' Use of Time

We saw the influence of the reassigned time for the group leaders as soon as they tried to document the time they allotted to teacher research leadership and how much to other responsibilities such as preparing for their teaching. Their teaching and research responsibilities were completely intermixed. While writing in a research log, for example, a teacher researcher leader would see a lesson plan emerge. While discussing a teaching problem with a fellow teacher researcher, a leader would have an idea for her own research. All three leaders were accustomed to thinking about teaching and researching in a variety of situations and places other than the few hours allotted to them at their desks at school.

Substitute Leave Time for the Teacher Researcher Network

The Network, which included teacher researcher leaders from schools other than the three in the project, provided members four substitute leave days to participate during the first year, but not all of those invited were able to attend. Their participation was not a priority at their schools and depended on the other professional obligations they had accepted for the year, the pressure of their teaching responsibilities, and their own personal interest in furthering the goals of the Network. In most cases these teacher leaders had the same responsibilities for a research group in their schools as the three teacher leaders in the project, but without the reassigned time to do the work. Difficulties in participating fully were directly related to the demands on their time.

Time for Project Planning and Decision Making

In the administrative office where Nocerino and Rogers worked, the expectation that time would be spent on the teacher research project was verified by the superintendent when he mentioned the project in his address at the opening of school. Still, more time was needed to direct the project than we originally anticipated because of our practice of shared decision making. A related reason was that the Planning Group was also a research group. We shared a commitment to research as a way of knowing and as a basis for action. Decisions about project administration were made by examination of accumulated data about the teachers, their research, the schools, and other issues related to the context in which the work was occurring.

TIME FOR TEACHER RESEARCH: IMPLICATIONS

All our data indicate that time given in support of teacher research in schools is a wise investment in teachers' professional development that results in increased student learning. Such an investment is dependent on the need for a long-term commitment by those who control the use of teachers' time, a commitment that recognizes the complexity of schools as organizations, the roles of teachers within their schools, and the ways in which school culture has traditionally resisted teacher knowledge and leadership. The very activity—conducting research—for which the time is needed, is not expected in a teacher's daily schedule. But with the glimpse of possibilities that we observed in three schools, we think the implications are persuasive for school districts to provide the time.

Much of the energy and momentum of the project depended on the modified teaching schedules funded for the three teacher researcher leaders. Their teaching and making use of the knowledge gained in their classrooms, their time to reflect and write, their flexibility to work with other teachers, their connections with school governance groups, their attendance at planning sessions during the school day, their attendance at professional conferences to give workshops based on their knowledge, are all features that describe the work of a professional. But actually, these features make them highly unusual members of the teaching profession. They are unusual not because they are dedicated teachers willing to work long hours, as do many teachers, but because they *had* time to work both in and beyond their classrooms as their knowledge and abilities warranted.

Reassigned time that significantly modifies a teacher's schedule is a problematic item in school budgets, although substitute leave time is sometimes offered for new programs. For a teacher, substitute leave offers precious time to work with colleagues, but takes away precious time to work with students and is an additional work load of preparation and follow-up. Reassigned time and modified schedules mean fewer classes to teach and fewer students—time during the school day for other professional activities.

We do not know what changes might occur in U.S. schools if teachers had time to prepare and plan, to reflect, research, and write. What tends to happen, especially to well-regarded teachers, is that they are given more work to do without modified schedules—more "difficult" students to teach, more student teachers to supervise, more committee and curriculum responsibilities—and often are encouraged to leave the classroom for administrative positions or a doctoral program leading out of teaching altogether. Then, it is assumed, they will be able to plan, reflect, research, and write with knowledge and authority.

Teachers who elect to remain in the classroom may be called dedicated, and they may be thanked. But they are not given time to have the most impact as *teachers*—to study the learning of their students, to grow professionally with colleagues, and to contribute to the improvement of their schools and profession through their research and accumulated knowledge. Our research strongly suggests that school systems are hampering and misdirecting their greatest asset, the work of teachers with students in class-rooms and with each other.

TEACHERS AS PROFESSIONALS: DISCUSSION

The teacher researchers in the project schools developed different ways of seeing themselves as learners and knowers. They made changes in their teaching as a result of what they found out as researchers, changes to increase the learning of their students.

Teachers as Researchers

With the support of the group leaders and their colleagues, the teacher researchers examined their teaching publicly and used the research process to exchange ideas and practices with each other. They worked in an atmosphere of trust so that they could face difficult questions and accept hard answers based on their own data.

They expressed views of themselves as people with ideas about teaching and learning to contribute to colleagues and with findings related to school program planning and evaluation and to district curriculum and policies. They became more knowledgeable readers of research in the professional literature and more interested in reading it.

Multiple Roles for Teacher Researcher Leaders

The teacher researcher leaders were simultaneously participating in project planning; conducting their own research projects; introducing colleagues to classroom research; learning to provide different kinds of leadership as the needs of the group changed; becoming more involved in disseminating research in the school system and beyond; and finally, but importantly, becoming involved in decision making at their schools as teacher research results became a part of the schools' knowledge base about learning. These multiple roles were anticipated—desired, in fact—but the teacher leaders involved, despite their extensive experience, understandably found it difficult to balance all of them.

Changing Definitions of Teacher Leadership

All three teacher researcher leaders were well respected as teachers by their colleagues and administrators, yet they still ran into traditional expectations. At issue were questions about the following:

- What were their responsibilities? Were they available to fill in for absent teachers? Could they be asked to help with teaching problems as well as with research?
- What space did they need? Since they were teaching fewer classes, did they need their own classroom workspace? If they were sometimes gone from the school building, could they be full members of middle school teams or other faculty groups?
- What relationship did they have with school administrators? Were they quasi administrators themselves? Did the administrators in their schools value them more highly than other teachers?

Professional Development

Teacher research groups in schools are not traditional staff development, and they work their way into the program of a school without a preset agenda. Teacher research is planned by teachers themselves and related to their interests and needs, which are, in turn, related to the interests and needs of their students and their schools. Because of these differences, the teacher research groups were in some cases in competition, if not conflict, with other professional development programs of their schools and school district.

Teachers in Professional Activities Beyond Their Schools

Attempts to involve teacher researchers from the project schools in professional activities such as the Teacher Researcher Network, conference presentations, or publication in state or national journals were not always successful. A number of school-based teacher researchers were unable or unwilling to take time away from their classes and students; they could not afford the travel and conference expenses; they did not see some of the conferences as relevant to their daily work; or they did not feel ready to report on their research after one year. Most were not accustomed to thinking of themselves as leaders within their own profession nor as researchers with ideas that matter to others beyond their schools.

TEACHERS AS PROFESSIONALS: IMPLICATIONS

Teacher researcher groups in schools affirm that teachers are capable of generating their own knowledge about teaching and learning and directing their own professional growth. Much professional development that exists in schools, however, comes from offices outside the school and personnel outside the classroom—from individuals who cannot fully know or appreciate the particular context in which students and teachers are learning and teaching. What such approaches to teacher professional development convey, intended or not, is a disregard for or mistrust of teacher knowledge. That message is not missed by teacher researchers.

Teachers' research groups become a welcome source of support, and they appreciate the opportunity for collaborative inquiry, the respect for diverse opinions, and the understanding of trusted colleagues. In her doctoral study of teacher research groups, Sharon Gerow, a high school teacher researcher in our district, described the development of trust in these groups: "The teachers' new knowledge and understanding came about because they engaged in lengthy, extensive periods of time for talk and deep conversations about children, research, and other relevant issues and because they reflected thoughtfully on how they practiced collaborative skills"(1997, p. 147).

If it works in their research groups, why not in other areas of the school's planning and evaluation? Judith Warren Little characterizes existing school cultures as follows: "School teaching has endured largely as an assemblage of entrepreneurial individuals whose autonomy is grounded in norms of privacy and noninterference and is sustained by the very organizing of teaching work" (1991, p. 530). Little says that there are few precedents for teacher leadership in collaborative efforts and that such a change in teacher culture offers teachers the possibility of even more criticism and conflict than is already present in their lives. That possibility is not missed by teacher researchers either.

But for the most part, the teacher researchers in our project welcomed the possibility of being more involved in the decisions that affected their classrooms. In a learning community of mutual respect such as a teacher research group, they saw that school decision making could be efficient, be data driven, and promote learning. They knew that such work would take time and worried that they would not be given the time to do the job well, but they saw it as a logical next step.

Teacher researchers, given a voice, have the potential to change the way knowledge about education is generated and what that knowledge is even beyond their schools. But to include teacher researchers in the acquisition of educational knowledge would also mean a change in the way teachers are viewed by their educational colleagues in administration and in colleges and universities. That is why teachers cannot make these changes alone. They need the support of their colleagues who are now the decision makers with power.

SCHOOL PLANNING AND EVALUATION: DISCUSSION

We saw that there could be a connection between teacher research and school planning and evaluation if teacher research were seen by school administrators as valuable and if school planning were seen as a way to involve teachers in decision making, using local knowledge to inform that decision making.

Differences Among the Three Schools

There were differences among the three schools in the effects of the teacher researcher groups. Although we did not study those differences in depth, we suspect that they were related to factors such as the following:

- Presence or absence of a tradition in the school of professional growth activities
- Attitudes toward professional development and professional organizations outside the school
- Size and organizational structure of the school
- Extent to which teachers had had experience working collaboratively toward instructional goals.

Other factors include unrelated but significant activities that demanded time and attention such as new school administrators, school renovations, and threatened school closings. The differences generally affected the visibility of the research findings disseminated by the teacher researchers and the steadiness of the research group's position as an expected and important part of the school's total program.

Teacher Research as Information for School Planning

Our past experience indicated that teachers must freely choose to do teacher research and that they must choose subjects that matter to them. What we saw happening in this project was that their choices of subjects mirrored the issues of the school at large. If the school was embarking on block scheduling, for example, teacher researchers wanted to know how it would affect their students' learning. If new curriculum was being introduced, teacher researchers wanted to investigate its implementation in their classes. Teacher researchers were involved in the life of the school and saw themselves as responsible to the school community.

Qualitative and Quantitative Data for School Planning and Evaluation

Schools need full and complete data on which to make decisions about programs and curriculum, and consequently, about budget and staffing. Quantitative data, such as standardized test results, absentee rates, or grade distributions, offer only part of the information needed. Such data do not explain the whys and hows of achievement or how to design or revise school programs and curriculum.

Qualitative data, the kind analyzed in most teacher research studies, provides the missing information that schools need. Miles and Huberman (1994) describe the relationship between quantitative and qualitative data by saying that qualitative data supplements, validates, explains, illuminates, or reinterprets quantitative data (p.10). Teacher research studies help interpret and explain the statistics and offer, in addition, practical views of teaching that can be of help to all teachers in a school. Teacher research studies also provide baseline information that goes beyond statistical measures of assessment to illuminate areas where the school can concentrate its improvement efforts in program and curriculum change.

Administrative Support for Teacher Research

School-based administrators recognize the potential of teacher researcher knowledge to inform teaching and learning. They also recognize teacher research groups as powerful professional development. In many districts, however, schools regularly experience turnover of administrators and teachers, making it difficult to develop leadership and establish a shared culture. Decisions about curriculum and professional development are made by people outside individual schools and school-based administrators feel this pressure as well as teachers.

SCHOOL PLANNING AND EVALUATION:
IMPLICATIONS

When a teacher research learning community is sustained in a school over time, it has the potential for changing the school culture into one fully focused on learning. What would a school that responded to the implications of our findings look like? In such a school we would expect to see the following features:

- Time provided for teachers to teach and learn with colleagues as they conduct research

- Time provided for teacher leaders to organize teacher research groups and support them as necessary
- Time provided for teacher leaders to develop and support professional development programs based on teacher research
- Recognition and use of research findings and skills developed by teacher researchers in school programs and governance
- A learning community of teachers providing themselves and their colleagues with classroom- and context-based information about teaching and learning in their school
- Administrators and teachers who recognize the links between teacher research and school goals and objectives, and who are organized to take advantage of the links so that many voices contribute to school planning

And what would the school district look like? Administrators and school boards would view teaching and learning in classrooms as the central focus of a school system from which knowledge about teaching and learning, in the form of teacher research, would inform the goals, programs, curriculum, and policies of the school district. It is in the school classrooms where the important things happen, but it is not classroom knowledge and experience that are currently fostered, respected, or included in decision making in most school districts.

We do not see teacher research as an "innovation" added to a school's program, as a teaching method or curriculum change might be, but as a way of viewing teaching and learning in classrooms resulting in a way of viewing professional development, school planning, and program evaluation. School boards, school reformers, school administrators, and those responsible for school budgets, if they are to promote school improvement, must look to teacher knowledge and teacher leadership as a strength of school systems, putting teaching and learning at the center of school decision making and giving teacher researchers the time and opportunity to work toward school improvement with each other and the administrators in their schools.

DIRECTIONS FOR THE FUTURE

In our school district, as in many nationwide, new measures of teaching and learning have been mandated. Legislators, school boards, and superintendents decide that the evaluation of teaching and learning will be by accumulated statistical measures, such as numbers of students enrolled in Advanced Placement courses and levels of scores on standardized tests. It is possible to see this as a direction that ignores or disparages teacher research, but we believe that it can also be an opportunity for teacher researchers to participate in the evaluation of learning in the schools. The question is how.

As a result of this project, many more teachers in our district learned how to conduct teacher research and how to lead groups of teacher researchers. The grant gave us "a critical mass of time and a critical mass of sustained effort to develop teacher research," Sanford noted, and we all agree. Some teacher researcher groups in the schools continue their work regardless of the institutional support or lack of it that they receive. Some seek support from their principals or other administrators.

But Rogers asked: "How long can teachers sustain leadership and support of teacher research if it's basically going against the grain of the environment—the school culture and school system?" Her question reminds us that the future holds some of the same challenges that we recognized before we began. The difference for us is similar to the difference for an individual teacher researcher in a classroom: Our thinking and understanding are not the same as they were at the beginning. We have new understandings about teaching, learning, and conducting teacher research in schools, and we want to express them in the best way possible and offer them to our colleagues in the ultimate hope of making a difference to the students in our classrooms.

REFERENCES

Gerow, S. (1997). *Teacher researchers in school-based collaborative teams: One approach to school reform.* Unpublished doctoral dissertation, Institute for Educational Transformation, George Mason University, Fairfax County, VA.

Little, J. W. (1991). The persistence of privacy: Autonomy and initiative in teachers' professional relations. *Teachers College Record, 91*(4), 509–536.

Miles, M., & Huberman, A. M. (1994). *Qualitative data analysis: An expanded sourcebook* (2nd. ed.). Beverly Hills, CA: Sage.

Stenhouse, L. (1985). *Research as a basis for teaching: Readings from the work of Lawrence Stenhouse* (J. Ruddick & D. Hopkins, eds.). Westport, CT: Heinemann-Boynton/Cook.

Bibliography

The following books and articles are an addition to those already listed as references at the ends of chapters. These works have been useful to us and give the reader more writers to explore on the subject of teacher research in schools.

Anderson, G. L., & Herr, K. (1999). The new paradigm wars: Is there room for rigorous practitioner knowledge in schools and universities? *Educational Researcher, 28*(5), 12–21, 40.

Anderson, G. L., Herr, K., & Nihlen, A. S. (1994). *Studying your own school: An educator's guide to qualitative practitioner research.* Thousand Oaks, CA: Corwin Press.

Anderson, P. V. (1998). Simple gifts: Ethical issues in the conduct of person-based composition research. *College Composition and Communication, 49*(1), 63–89.

Athanases, S. Z., & Heath, S. B. (1995). Ethnography in the study of the teaching and learning of English. *Research in the Teaching of English, 29*(3), 263–287.

Atwell, N. (1990). Wonderings to pursue: The writing teacher as researcher. In B. M. Power & R. Hubbard (Eds.), *Literacy in process* (pp. 315–331). Portsmouth, NH: Heinemann-Boynton/Cook.

Ballenger, C. (1992). Because you like us: The language of control. *Harvard Educational Review, 62*(2), 199–208.

Berthoff, A. (1981). *The making of meaning.* Portsmouth, NH: Heinemann-Boynton/Cook.

Bogdan, R., & Biklin, S. (1992). *Qualitative research for education: An introduction to theory and methods* (2nd ed.). Boston: Allyn and Bacon.

Burton, F. R. (1986). Research currents: A teacher's conception of the action research process. *Language Arts, 63*(7), 718–723.

Carmichael, C. (1998). Mi voz suena asi (My voice sounds like this): Generative themes in second grade. *The Quarterly of the National Writing Project, 20*(4), 13–20.

Christian, S. (1995, Fall/Winter). School reform and teacher research. *Bread Loaf Rural Teacher Network Magazine* (Middlebury College), pp. 32–33.

Clawson, S. (1993). The impact of collaborative writing on the individual. *Teaching and Change, 1*(1), 55–69.

Cochran-Smith, M., & Lytle, S. L. (1999). The teacher research movement: A decade later. *Educational Researcher, 28*(7), 15–25.

Darling-Hammond, L. (1996). The quiet revolution: Rethinking teacher development. *Educational Leadership, 53*(6), 4–10.

Donoahue, Z., Van Tassell, M. A., & Patterson, L. (1996). *Research in the classroom: Talk, texts, and inquiry.* Newark, DE: International Reading Association.

Ellison, V. L. (1996). Having students select spelling words. *Teaching and Change, 4*(1), 77–89.

Ely, M., Anzul, M., Friedman, T., Garner, D., & Steinmetz, A. M. (1991). *Doing qualitative research: Circles within circles.* London: Falmer.

Fecho, R. (2001). "Why are you doing this?": Acknowledging and transcending threat in a critical inquiry classroom. *Research in the Teaching of English, 36*(1), 9–37.

Geertz, C. (1983). *Local knowledge: Further essays in interpretive anthropology.* New York: Basic Books.

Glaze, B. (1987). A teacher speaks out about research. In *Plain talk about learning and writing across the curriculum* (pp. 87–99). Richmond, VA: Virginia Department of Education, Production and Publication Committee.

Goetz, J., & LeCompte, M. (1984). *Ethnography and qualitative design in educational research.* Orlando, FL: Academic Press.

Graham, P., & Hudson-Ross, S. (with Adkins, C., Callaway, D., Wallace, J., Schwartz, J., & Solheim, K.). (2001). Collaborative teacher education for the 21st century. *English Education, 33*(2), 126–135.

Hermann, K., Carstarphen, N., & Coolidge, J. O. (1997). Meeting the challenges of diversity and conflict: The immigrant student experience. *Teaching and Change, 4*(3), 206–226.

Huberman, M. (1996). Moving mainstream: Taking a closer look at teacher research. *Language Arts, 73*(2), 124–140.

Ingalls, R. (1999). Learning school: Learning to write. In M. S. MacLean & M. M. Mohr, *Teacher-researchers at work* (pp. 169–179). Berkeley, CA: National Writing Project.

Johnson, R. (1993). Where can teacher research lead? One teacher's daydream. *Educational Leadership, 51*(2), 66–68.

LeCompte, M. (1987). Bias in biography: Bias and subjectivity in ethnographic research. *Anthropology and Education Quarterly, 18*(1), 43–52.

Lee, C. (2001). Is October Brown Chinese? A cultural modeling activity system for underachieving students. *American Educational Research Journal, 38*(1), 97–141.

Lofland, J., & Lofland, L. (1984). *Analyzing social settings: A guide to qualitative observation and analysis* (2nd ed.). Belmont, CA: Wadsworth.

MacLean, M. S. (1983). Voices within: The audience speaks. *English Journal, 72*(7), 62–66.

MacLean, M. S., & Mohr, M. M. (1999). *Teacher-researchers at work.* Berkeley, CA: National Writing Project.

Miller, J. (1990). *Creating spaces and finding voices: Teachers collaborating for empowerment.* Albany: State University of New York Press.

Mishler, E. G. (1990). Validation in inquiry-guided research: The role of exemplars in narrative studies. *Harvard Educational Review, 60*(4), 415–442.

Mohr, M. M. (1980). The teacher as researcher. *Virginia English Bulletin, 30*(2), 61–64.

Mohr, M. M. (1984). *Revision: The rhythm of meaning.* Portsmouth, NH: Heinemann-Boynton/Cook.

Mohr, M. M., & MacLean, M. S. (1987). *Working together: A guide for teacher researchers.* Urbana, IL: National Council of Teachers of English.

Mortensen, P., & Kirsch, G. E. (1996). *Ethics and representation in qualitative studies of literacy.* Urbana, IL: National Council of Teachers of English.

Nocerino, M. A. (1993). A look at the process. In L. Patterson, C. Santa, K. G. Short, & K. Smith (Eds.), *Teachers are researchers: Reflection and action* (pp. 86–91). Newark, DE: International Reading Association.

Ozvold, L. A. (1996). Does teacher demeanor affect the behavior of students? *Teaching and Change, 3*(2), 159–172.

Paley, V. G. (1992). *You can't say you can't play.* Cambridge, MA: Harvard University Press.

Patterson, L., Santa, C., Short, K. G., & Smith, K. (1993). *Teachers are researchers: Reflection and action.* Newark, DE; International Reading Association.

Perl, S., & Wilson, N. (1986). *Through teachers' eyes: Portraits of writing teachers at work.* Portsmouth, NH: Heinemann.

Polanyi, M. (1962). *Personal knowledge: Toward a post-critical philosophy.* Chicago: University of Chicago Press.

Polanyi, M., & Prosch, H. (1975). *Meaning.* Chicago: University of Chicago Press.

Rogers, C. (1989). A teacher-researcher writes about learning. In M. M. Mohr & M. S. MacLean, *Working together: A guide for teacher researchers* (pp. 94–102). Urbana, IL: National Council of Teachers of English.

Sanford, B. (1987). Discovering revision. In M. M. Mohr & M. S. MacLean, *Working together: A guide for teacher researchers* (pp. 102–111). Urbana, IL: National Council of Teachers of English.

Schaafsma, D., Tendero, A., & Tendero, J. (1999). Making it real: Girls' stories, social change, and moral struggle. *English Journal, 88*(5), 28–37.

Schön, D. (1983). *The reflective practitioner: How professionals think in action.* New York: Basic Books.

Shafer, L. (1995). Anecdotal record keeping: Learning from Rosa, Ahmed, and Zhou. *Journal* (Greater Washington Reading Council) *19*, 16–23.

Shaffner, A. (1997). Rubrics in middle school: Rewarding or rueful. *Teaching and Change, 4*(3), 258–283.

Spence, L. (1986). Gaining control through commentary. *English Journal, 75*(3), 58–62.

Spradley, J. (1979). *The ethnographic interview.* New York: Holt, Rinehart & Winston.

Stock, P. L. (2001). Toward a theory of genre in teacher research: Contributions from a reflective practitioner. *English Education, 33*(2), 100–114.

Swaim, M. S., & Swaim, S. C. (1999). *Teacher time.* Arlington, VA: Redbud Books.

Taylor, D. L., & Bogotch, I. E.(1994). School-level effects of teachers' participation in decision making. *Educational Evaluation and Policy Analysis, 16*(3), 302–319.

Wells, G., Bernard, L., Gianotti, M. A., Keating, C., Konjevic, C., Kowal, M., Maher, A., Mayer, C., Moscoe, T., Orzechowska, E., Smieja, A., & Swartz, L. (1994). *Changing schools from within: Creating communities of inquiry.* Toronto, Canada: OISE Press.

Wolcott, H. F. (1990). *Writing up qualitative research.* Qualitative Research Methods Series, No. 20. Newbury Park, CA: Sage.

Zeni, J. (Ed.). (2000). *Ethical issues in practitioner inquiry.* New York: Teachers College Press.

Index

About the Authors

Sheila Clawson teaches at Kilmer Middle School. She began her career as a language arts teacher at the elementary level. She has designed curriculum for gifted students, served as an instructor for the Johnson and Johnson model of cooperative learning, and taught English, French, social studies, technology, keyboarding, and creative writing at the middle school level. A teacher-consultant, first of the Duke Writing Project and subsequently of the Northern Virginia Writing Project, she has been conducting teacher research since 1985 and has published several studies.

Marion S. MacLean teaches at Thomas Jefferson High School for Science and Technology. She has been a high school English teacher, a writing resource teacher, and a district curriculum specialist. She became a teacher-consultant with the Northern Virginia Writing Project in 1981 and has served on its board of directors. MacLean has conducted and published several teacher research studies and is currently a trustee of the National Council of Teachers of English (NCTE) Research Foundation. With Mohr, she has published two books about conducting teacher research: *Working Together: A Guide for Teacher Researchers* (1987) and *Teacher-Researchers at Work* (1999).

Marian Mohr is retired from high school English teaching and works with school systems to establish and sustain teacher researcher groups and networks. In 1978 Mohr became a teacher-consultant with the Northern Virginia Writing Project, served as its codirector, and also as a member of the Advisory Board of the National Writing Project. She has been a member of the Standing Committee on Research of the National Council of Teachers of English and a trustee of the NCTE Research Foundation. She published her classroom research in *Revision: The Rhythm of Meaning* (1984), and with MacLean published two books on conducting teacher research: *Working Together: A Guide for Teacher Researchers* (1987) and *Teacher-Researchers at Work* (1999).

Mary Ann Nocerino began her career as an elementary and preschool Montessori teacher; later became a school-based reading specialist; and served in the Office of Planning, Testing, and Evaluation, a district central office, where she assisted schools in planning and program evaluation and in supporting school teacher research groups. Nocerino has been a Northern Virginia Writing Project teacher-consultant since 1980 and served as a member of the board of directors for over 10 years. She helped create the district's annual teacher researcher conference. Recently retired from the school system, she continues to work with schools in the field of school planning, program evaluation, and teacher research. She has published articles of and about teacher research.

Courtney Rogers teaches English at Falls Church High School. She was a school-based writing resource teacher and a language arts resource teacher for elementary and secondary schools. She worked with Nocerino in the Office of Planning, Testing, and Evaluation, supporting teachers and administrators as they planned and evaluated their school improvement efforts. A teacher-consultant for the Northern Virginia Writing Project since 1978, she first conducted teacher research in 1982. She has worked over the past several years with school-based teacher researcher groups and has helped to support the districtwide network of teacher researchers.

Betsy Sanford teaches at Lemon Road Elementary School, originally as a classroom teacher and more recently as a mathematics resource teacher. Her initial involvement with teacher research was in 1984 when she published her study of how fourth graders revise their writing. She became a teacher-consultant with the Northern Virginia Writing Project in 1986. She continues to conduct classroom research, increasingly on mathematics learning, and has helped support school-based teacher researcher groups. She has been co-chair of the Teacher Researcher Network and chaired the district's annual teacher researcher conference.